Coping with Dementia

Thoughts on the philosophy, principles, and practice of person-centered compassionate care.

P.O. Box 434
Inverness, FL 34451
www.dementiaedu.org

First Printing, February 2022

ISBN-13: 9798427987127

For information on purchasing this book
call 614-519-2843
dementiaed@aol.com
www.dementiaedu.org

Coping with Dementia

Thoughts on the philosophy,
principles, and practice
of person-centered
compassionate care.

By Debbie Selsavage, CDP

Edited by Ed Youngblood
Composition by Ruben Youngblood
Cover design by Joanne Crowley

DEMENTIAEDUCATION,INC.
A Citrus County Florida nonprofit

P.O. Box 434
Inverness, FL 34451
www.dementiaedu.org

Inspiration

I will remember that there is art to medicine as well as science, and that warmth, sympathy, and understanding may outweigh the surgeon's knife or the chemist's drug.

From the Modern Hippocratic Oath

I've learned that people will forget what you said, people will forget what you did, but people will never forget how you made them feel.

Maya Angelou

Until there's a cure, there is care.

Teepa Snow

Dedication

What I have learned over the decade since I lost my husband Albert to dementia is, sadly, that our experience was not atypical. The only thing our diagnosing physician could tell me was, "Hang on for the ride!" and few "experts" I spoke with after that were much more helpful.

Albert, whom I had always known as a gentle man, was labeled "combative" in the first memory care community to which he was admitted, and this began a process that included heavy application of mind-numbing psychotropics, rejection from three other communities, involuntary incarceration in a psychiatric facility where he was physically abused, hand-cuffed and placed in four-point restraints, and at one point returned to me in a taxi, dirty and ungroomed, wearing no shoes and someone else's clothing.

But I am one of the lucky ones. Near the end of Albert's life, I discovered a community that practiced person-centered compassionate care. This gave Albert happy and unmedicated serenity for a few months before his death, but it gave me a call to action that utterly changed my life. I felt strongly that thousands of other care partners like myself deserved to know that there is a better way.

This series of essays is dedicated to the millions of care partners – both lay persons and professionals – who seek to learn the philosophy and techniques that will change a still-medieval attitude toward dementia into the happier, humane, and more fulfilling practice of person-centered compassionate care.

--Debbie Selsavage, CDP

Introduction

When Debbie Selsavage formed Coping with Dementia LLC in 2014, two of its goals were 1) to promote and train care partners in the methods of person-centered compassionate care, a methodology and philosophy that had been denied her husband until the final months before his death in 2010; and 2) help erase the stigma and misunderstandings associated with dementia by creating a healthy and helpful public conversation about Alzheimer's disease and other forms of dementia; factual and free from fear.

One of the most fortunate developments in fulfillment of these goals came late in 2015 when the Citrus County Chronicle agreed to provide space for a monthly column, which Selsavage would provide on a voluntary and uncompensated basis. Entitled "Coping with Dementia," this column has appeared uninterrupted since January, 2016, and has proven so popular that several other print and on-line publications in and around Citrus County have asked to re-publish it.

While these writings have been archived at Chronicleonline.com and Coping.today, in late 2020, the nonprofit Dementia Education Inc. thought it advisable to make a majority of the body of work available in book form for family care partners, care professionals, and others who want to better understand the compassionate techniques of dementia care.

Selsavage always writes in plain language, never talks down to her readers, and often shares the hopeful and helpful experiences from the hundreds of participants she meets in her weekly on-line care partner support groups and her ABC of Dementia workshops.

This volume contains six years of Debbie's columns containing her thoughts on the philosophy, principles, and practices of person-centered compassionate care. As a Certified Dementia Practitioner and an Independent Trainer and Consultant in Teepa Snow's Positive Approach to Care®, she shares with us the ways to achieve a better quality of life while recognizing the moments of joy within the difficult journey of dementia.

Table of Contents

Chapter One:
The disease of our time

What is the difference between Alzheimer's and dementia?

This is one of the most frequent questions I hear. Dementia refers to a group of symptoms that includes memory loss, reduction in sensory perception such as vision and hearing, loss of motor skills, and loss of cognitive ability. There are many causes of dementia, but Alzheimer's is the greatest single cause of the common dementia symptoms. For our purposes, we will not labor the point; on a practical level, all causes of dementia have the same tragic result, usually with devastating effects on both individuals with dementia and their families.

With our current medical knowledge, there are some key facts we need to recognize about this disease:

> *It is currently incurable.
> *It is progressive.
> *It is irreversible.
> *It is fatal.
> *And it is the disease of our time and is going to get worse.

While death from heart disease and cancer declined 1.6 and 1.2 percent respectively from 2013 to 2014, death diagnosed due to Alzheimer's increased 8.1% in the same period. This trend will continue and accelerate.

The number of Americans with Alzheimer's disease and dementia is projected to soar to 7.1 million by 2025; a 40 percent increase from the 5.1 million affected now. By 2050, it is projected that in the United States there will be 13.8 million people with dementia.

This trend is in part due to longer lifespan. By 2040, the percentage of seniors will grow from one-fifth to one-quarter of our national population as Baby Boomers move into old age. But the threat is proportionately greater for Citrus County since we currently have almost double the Florida average for individuals over the age of 65!

Since Alzheimer's is currently incurable, do we just throw up our hands in despair? No, with no cure or remediation at hand, the most important thing we can do is focus on comfort, quality of life, and quality of care. Dementia individuals are not just insentient beings to be warehoused in institutions. They are not just old folks who refuse to behave. And though they are cognitively disadvantaged, they are not stupid. They are people who have unique histories and personalities, and who still have feelings.

In recent years, great strides have been made in the understanding of behaviors among individuals with Alzheimer's and other forms of dementia. Techniques have been developed to better communicate, motivate, and interact with them. These techniques are all grounded in patience, understanding, and compassion. They can easily be incorporated into improved care on a large scale, though I believe we are currently way behind the curve in this area of learning. Much more needs to be done in the application of person-centered compassionate care.

Next month, I will tell you my story and how I became an advocate for improved person-centered compassionate care for individuals with Alzheimer's and dementia, including ways to reduce the suffering experienced by their care partners and families. Then, in subsequent months we will discuss many topics related to dementia and better techniques of care.

But I want this to be your column too. I want it to be interactive. Please e-mail me your questions at deb@coping.today. I'll do my best to answer, and, if appropriate, share these answers with others through this column.

Until next month, remember my slogan: *We all deserve the best!*

Chapter Two:
My introduction to the dementia

Last month, I wrote about how dementia has become the disease of our time. I said then that I would explain how I became so interested in this problem and why I believe we must implement different and better standards of care.

I'm not telling my story because I think it is special or unique. Sadly, and to the contrary, it is a very common story that tens of thousands have played out in one version or another. My introduction to Alzheimer's came when I found myself a care partner, whether I liked it or not.

In 2004, my husband, Albert, a 68-year-old very healthy and active man who bicycled 25 miles a day, began to exhibit personality changes. In May that year, we were on a trip, and he became lost in a hotel. The staff had to bring him to our room. On that same trip, he became temperamental and angry, shouting and using abusive language. This was not normal or characteristic behavior.

Two months later he was diagnosed with Alzheimer's, began to have difficulty with dexterity and motor skills, and soon lost his ability to speak. I was working full-time but managed to care for him until late 2008. That summer he began to wander, and I could no longer leave him alone during the day.

By early 2009, I had to place him in an assisted living facility (ALF) where he lasted only three days because they said he was angry and combative. They had no idea how to deal with him, so he was 'Baker Acted.' This means he was involuntarily committed to a psychiatric hospital where he stayed for a week, and I was not allowed to visit him.

When he was released, he had no shoes and was wearing someone else's clothes. Defecation was dried to him, and he was covered with bruises. He was sent to another ALF, and by 6:30 the next morning they were threatening to Baker Act him again.

The next months were spent trying to find a facility that would care for Albert, then repeating the process when they too threatened to Baker Act. This shuttling from one facility to another included twelve weeks in a psychiatric hospital where he was often kept in four-point restraints. I was exhausted and at my wits' end. Many mornings I would break down sobbing, then suck it up and go to work where I pretended nothing was wrong.

Finally, I found a small six-bed facility where the administrator/owner told me that Albert would never be required to move again. She said, "Don't you worry; we will love him through this." I had no idea what she was talking about. I had never heard anyone connected with dementia care use the word "love." But I saw it actually work. She and her staff were calm, kind, compassionate, and loving. Force was never used and voices were never raised. Albert's personality calmed, his disruptive behavior ended, and he lived there in apparent tranquility for the next four months before he died.

This long nightmare and its good ending taught me many things about coping with dementia. I learned that "the system" is woefully under-trained to effectively care for people with dementia. But I was exposed to a better way based on compassion, love, and respect for a person's dignity.

Part of my problem was that I could just not find the resources I needed. I was operating alone and in the dark. This situation has improved since 2010. There is greater awareness about Alzheimer's and dementia, there are more family support groups, and there are more resources available to care partners. Still, though, we have a long way to go.

During most of my ordeal, I longed for a day when I would never hear the word "Alzheimer's" again. But those final months changed my outlook and eventually my life's journey. I had been shown a better way. I became licensed by the State of Florida as an ALF administrator and became a certified trainer in Teepa Show's Positive Approach to Care®. I also became a Certified Dementia Practitioner and eventually earned other certifications in the Snow Approach.

In 2014, I formed Coping with Dementia LLC, a company dedicated to promoting dementia awareness and higher standards of care that can be learned by both professional and lay care partners. My goal is that in the future fewer people will have to go through the trial I went through.

There is so much we have to talk about in the coming months, most of which will be focused on ways to give persons with dementia a better quality of life while easing the stress on you, the care partner. I know it will work because I have seen it work.

Please e-mail me your questions at deb@coping.today. I'll answer you personally and, if appropriate, share these answers with others through this column.

Until next month, remember my slogan: *We all deserve the best!*

Chapter Three:
The possible signs of dementia

One of the most common misunderstandings about Alzheimer's and other causes of dementia is that it involves only memory loss. Memory loss is a key and conspicuous symptom, but dementia causes many other physiological and neurological changes that can result in changes in behavior.

First, let me offer a reassurance that forgetting things does not mean you have dementia. It happens to all of us. "Where are my keys?" "Where did I leave my coat?" "Oh gosh, I'm so embarrassed; I can't remember this guy's name?" Relax, there's about a 90 percent chance you *don't* have dementia.

An individual with abnormal memory loss will begin to repeat him or herself, often asking questions you have just recently answered. Short-term memory is affected first. A person with dementia may recall events from the past, but not remember what they did an hour ago. Eventually, even long-term memory will be affected.

Having trouble with familiar and once easy tasks can be an indicator of dementia. For example, managing money, remembering medications, or driving safely are examples. This can result from both cognitive and physical changes. For example, motor skills will decline and a person with dementia may find it difficult to button a shirt or tie his shoes.

Forgetting common words or miss-naming things can suggest encroaching dementia. Did you see the movie "Still Alice?" Suddenly, Alice was unable to remember the word "lexicon," which described the very core of her profession as a Ph.D. Professor in linguistics.

Confusion as to time and place can be a symptom. This, combined with degraded judgment and motor skills, is why it is so dangerous for a person with dementia to continue to drive or have access to firearms.

Degraded judgment can include not thinking things through or jumping to unwarranted conclusions. This can include paranoia. Remember our talking about losing your keys? A normal person will begin to mentally retrace his steps in a logical process. A person with dementia may immediately jump to the conclusion that someone has stolen his keys. Paranoia and confusion may cause a person with dementia to place things in odd and unusual places, such as their car keys in the freezer! They may begin to hoard and create hiding places where they tuck things away.

Noticeable changes in personality, mood, and behavior can be caused by dementia. This may be exhibited in a loss of initiative when the person with dementia loses interest in the things he has enjoyed. Someone with dementia may show fear, frustration, and anger at an uncharacteristic level.

Because dementia is progressive, irreversible, and currently incurable, it has become the most feared malady of our time. If you or a loved one exhibits some of the behaviors described above, A) Don't panic and jump to conclusions, and B) Don't withdraw into denial. These extreme and opposite reactions are not helpful.

First, be aware that some of these symptoms can be caused by detectible and curable medical conditions. For example, thyroid gland malfunction and urinary tract infection can result in dementia-like behaviors. These are relatively easy problems to deal with.

This is why the proper reaction to concerns about abnormal behaviors and loss of memory is screening and diagnosis as early as possible. You may be able to rule out dementia. Finding that your problem is not dementia, but something correctable, will give you and your family immeasurable peace of mind.

And, if screening results in a diagnosis of dementia, it is good to know early because there are medications and therapies that can benefit the quality of life during the progress of the disease.

If you have questions, please e-mail me at deb@coping.today. I'll answer you personally and, if appropriate, share these answers with others through this column.

Until next month, remember my slogan: *We all deserve the best!*

Chapter Four:
Peer Support: When do we seek help?

Last year I was contacted by a woman who wanted to talk about her role as a care partner for a husband with Alzheimer's disease. Turns out, she and a circle of friends who were in similar situations had already formed a support group. When I learned this, I suggested we all get together for lunch, and soon I found myself at a table with nine women, all of whom were providing care for a loved one with dementia.

We discussed the fact that an Alzheimer's diagnosis is a terminal diagnosis, and what this means on emotional and practical levels. The fact that your loved one is not going to get better must be dealt with. You cannot predict how quickly dementia will progress, so you need to handle the legal aspects without delay. Become their advocate by obtaining a Durable Power of Attorney that includes health care, immediately! This is necessary so you can continue to participate in your loved one's care.

No terminal diagnosis is easy to deal with, but with most other diseases, the person remains lucid. The loved one can share his (her) feelings and rationally discuss how to get their affairs in order. With dementia, it has often progressed enough that your loved one really can't contribute to the necessary decisions about care, so you often carry the burden alone. This is why you should seek peer support. In a group you will share knowledge and discuss solutions.

Our luncheon group also had a frank discussion about medical support. I learned that in many cases, care partners were dealing solely with their primary care physician. Some said the only advice they received was, "Put him away immediately," meaning you should find a nursing home or assisted living community now because you won't be able to deal with it. I don't necessarily subscribe to this advice. Every case is different, and you might be able to use home health support for a long time.

Dementia is a complex area of medicine, and our body of knowledge and research is growing rapidly. There are medications available that can reduce anxiety and quell destructive behaviors. It is also good to consult a psychiatrist who specializes in dementia to seek information your primary care physician may not be trained to provide.

In the case of our luncheon group, all were still caring for their loved ones at home, and of course the question arose, "How do I know when it is time to turn my loved one over to assisted living?" There is no pat answer to this, but I replied that your loved one's behavior will tell you. If he (she) wanders and comes into dangerous situations; if incontinence becomes unmanageable; if he (she) is not sleeping or refuses to let you administer meds; or if your loved one becomes combative; these are the very clear signs that you can benefit from outside support.

We also discussed the fact that you must be kind to yourself; you must take care of yourself. If you become exhausted and so frustrated that you can no longer respond to your loved one with understanding and compassion, it is time to get help, not just for him or her but also for you. When you are stretched beyond your patience, energy, and emotional resources, you are beyond providing the care that your loved one deserves.

Again, seek out a peer group that is knowledgeable, supportive, and positive. If you have friends or relatives who tend to guilt you for not doing enough, gravitate away from them. You definitely don't need this kind of "help." Perhaps that relationship can return to normal later.

I hear so many care partners say, "I will never put him in an institution!" I assure you, this may be a hard promise to keep, and it may not be a promise that is beneficial to either of you. Sometimes an assisted living facility will become a "community" where your loved one will find comfort and friendship among peers. It can result in a better quality of life for both of you.

Next month we'll discuss the kinds of outside help that are available, and how to choose the level of support you need.

Until then, please remember our slogan: *"We all deserve the best."*

Chapter Five:
Wandering is a clear
and present danger

I have some friends who have a toddler. They recently invited me over to see their new swimming pool. I was astonished because there was no fence around the pool, so I asked the husband, "Don't you need a fence to protect your child?" He said, "What for? He hasn't fallen yet."

Sorry, that's not a true story. I made it up, but it is exactly the kind of logic I have heard many times from care partners when I warn them about the dangers of wandering. I've heard them say, "We don't have a problem. He hasn't wandered yet."

It is almost inevitable that people with dementia will wander, and we must have countermeasures to keep them safe. Six out of ten people who wander will get lost, and if not found within 24 hours there is a good chance that death will be the outcome. Wandering is very dangerous under any circumstances, but especially in Citrus County where we have jungle-like vegetation, many lakes and wetlands, and lots of drainage retention areas.

A wandering person immediately finds himself in an alien environment. There will be unfamiliar landmarks, noise, possibly traffic, and other distractions. They are likely to become frightened and more confused, and may hide. In this state of mind, calling their name is not likely to get results. Recruit assistance – such as the Sheriff's Department – as quickly as possible because the amount of time that passes only increases the likelihood of a bad outcome.

There are many products that can be used to reduce the likelihood of wandering, or to improve the chance that those who wander will be found. A bracelet with the individual's name and a number to call is advisable. There are more sophisticated products such as GPS monitors – like an ankle bracelet – that can be activated with your cell phone; but these can be expensive.

You can put electronic alarms on your doors so you will immediately hear when someone exits the house. You can put locks out of sight at the tops or bottoms of doors that the dementia person is not likely to notice or be able to operate. However, never ever leave your loved one locked in alone when you are gone.

It is dangerous and, in most jurisdictions, illegal!

I strongly recommend a simple and inexpensive product called a Human Scent Preservation Kit – Scent Kit for short -- that can help in locating a missing person. It is a sterile jar that will hold a gauze or fabric containing the pure scent of a person. Having this kit will allow a special unit of bloodhounds to trace your loved one (this is a great idea for children as well).

Just a few months ago, we had a rescue here in Citrus County, thanks to a scent kit. A man with dementia wandered off during the night. Fortunately, his wife had preserved her husband's unique scent. When she realized he was gone from the home, she called the Sheriff's office which responded with searchers and even a helicopter.

When a bloodhound trainer and handler arrived, they opened the Scent Kit jar and the dog went to work. Within five minutes, she found the man, hiding in the bushes under the roof overhang of the house next door. He was in a place, right there nearby, where the helicopter crew could not possibly see him and where foot searchers had not noticed. Possibly, a life had been saved.

Chapter Six:
Recognizing dementia behaviors

Previously, we discussed what Alzheimer's and dementia can do to a person. People think of it as a "memory" disease, but in fact a lot more than memory is affected. Dementia also effects vision, auditory and olfactory abilities, the ability to reason, judgment, and motor skills. The combination of these deficits can result in what many consider strange and unsettling behaviors.

Outbursts are one of the ways dementia sufferers respond to fear and frustration. Perhaps they realize that not long ago they could deal with a simple daily task, but now they cannot. They simply cannot remember how to solve a small problem, and this frightens them. They may explode in a temper tantrum, throw things, or even try to kick, hit, or bite their care partner. Try to remember that these are not just people behaving badly. Their behavior, driven by the disease, is beyond their control and could be telling you something. We can learn to respond in helpful ways.

Outbursts, and many other negative behaviors can be caused by too much stimulation, time of day, or too many choices. The levels of noise, distraction, and choices that you live with daily – and that your loved one coped with not long ago – have just become too much to handle. Try to eliminate overstimulation and the number of options your loved one must face.

Layering clothing, for example, is another odd but common behavior. They put on two pair of pants, layers of shirts, a coat over another coat, etc. This is likely the result of too many choices. Don't throw open the closet and say "It's time to get dressed." That closet full of clothes is simply overwhelming. Limit the choices to the articles of clothes your loved one should wear that day, and if they still struggle, help them with love, patience, and understanding.

Hoarding things and compulsive organization can be another behavior of a person with dementia. One day, I learned to my dismay that my husband Albert had not been taking his medication. Instead, he had been hoarding pills on a very high shelf in the closet, carefully lining them up in a long row.

Even in advanced stages of dementia, memory care patients have a sense of what is "their stuff," and they want to protect it from loss or someone else taking it. This behavior is associated with paranoia. Sometimes they may have lost something important to them, and they believe someone else has taken it. So, they respond by hoarding, hiding, and protecting things.

One of the most dangerous behaviors is "exit seeking." They will leave the house and wander, perhaps looking for someone or someplace still living in their long-term memory. This behavior requires planning and safeguards. Last month my column discussed the use of a Human Scent Preservation Kit to help scent-discriminating dogs find a person who has wandered and become lost. Currently, these are free in Citrus County.

Many people with dementia experience "sundowning," when the end of the day is their most emotionally difficult time. The troubling behaviors they perform during the day will only become worse at this time. Again, remember that it is the disease. They are not trying to be difficult. Reduce stimulation, turn on lights, lower the shades, try soothing music.

Pay attention to when behaviors happen. Most people with dementia have a time of day that is better, and a time that is worse, and this is usually predictable. Maintaining a routine is important, so don't schedule the more difficult tasks, such as bathing, during their bad time of day.

As a general rule in dealing with all disturbing behaviors, reduce stimulation, limit choices, and most of all respond with patience, love, and understanding. Scolding and saying "How many times have we gone over this . . ." will only make matters worse. We must recognize and suppress our own frustration that causes harsh reactions.

Try to shift your focus from your own frustration to what your loved one must be feeling to behave as they do. If you can do this – and it is not easy – you can replace frustration with compassion. Love, compassion, and understanding are the best tools you have in dealing with this disease and protecting your own sanity.

And don't forget, *"We all deserve the best!"* This slogan applies both to you and the person you are caring for.

Chapter Seven:
What can you do
when the truth hurts?

This month we are going to tackle a difficult topic. But it is important because it is one of the most common problems in the relationship between a care partner and their loved one with Alzheimer's or dementia.

What do you say when your loved one asks a question for which the real-world, literal, direct, factual, answer can only cause them more confusion and pain? This happens frequently, and as a frequent occurrence, it is an issue you must be prepared to deal with in a way that hopefully will not violate your own sense of honesty and integrity.

As we have mentioned before, individuals with dementia often seem to dwell in a period from their past. They can be relatively lucid about memories, events, and relationships from days long gone. This is their reality, and in this reality there are relatives and friends who have long since passed on. They will ask you about them – *Where's Bill?*; *Why hasn't my mother called?*; *What is Jill doing today*? – and you must be prepared to respond, knowing that the factual answer can only cause more confusion, grief, and pain.

There are few pat answers in dealing with Alzheimer's and dementia. Every case is different, and every relationship is unique, and we must seek solutions that are as comfortable as possible for the loved one who is suffering from this awful disease. Some of my solutions may not work for you. You must find your own way, but I am going to suggest that whatever you work out, try to adhere to the underlying principle that you should *do no harm*. When you know the truth is going to hurt, I believe you should err toward avoiding pain, not toward telling "the truth" as it exists in your reality.

While I know not all readers will agree with me, in the case of an issue of no real consequence, I believe there is nothing wrong with a "little white lie." Let me give you an example. One day a woman at a community I administered was becoming agitated and asked, "Have you seen my car?" She had not driven a car in years, and I simply said, "Oh, yes, I parked it for you. The keys are in my purse. I'll get them for you later." She settled down and dropped the subject. End of problem.

The alternative might have been to respond, "Come on Judy! You know you don't have a car! Just settle down and forget about it!" I promise you; this would be a very foolish way to respond. You are not going to convince her she doesn't own a car. This will certainly take her to higher levels of anxiety, and she may even decide that there is a conspiracy to steal or deprive her of her car and that you are involved. Never risk destroying trust over a minor issue like this for the sake of telling "the truth."

Handling the problem becomes much more difficult for the care partner if it involves seeking friends and relatives who are no longer with us. This happens often: *Have you seen my father today? Where is my husband?*" I've seen care partners respond in anger and frustration, "*Now mother, stop that, you know dad's been dead for 15 years!*" In my opinion, this kind of response is wrong, cruel, and very unhelpful.

Seeking a way to do no harm, some care partners may respond, "I think he may be coming by later." This is not the truth, but the objective here is not to tell the hurtful truth. The objective is to move the loved one's mind on to another topic while trying to do no harm.

Sometimes it works, and sometimes it doesn't, but the effort to do no harm is essential and commendable.

But what do you do when your own moral standards forbid you from telling even the whitest of little white lies? I know a woman – a nurse – with a lot of experience and wisdom in this field who in such cases will respond, "I have not seen him today. I'll let you know if I do." This is the literal truth, but it also can be effective in calming the loved one and moving her (his) thoughts on to another topic.

I think an even better way is to redirect the topic to reminiscence. "I know you really like Bill. I do too. Tell me some of the things you enjoy doing with him." This allows your loved one to address the memory in a pleasant and reassuring way without directly addressing the question. I have seen it work many times.

In caring for a loved one with dementia, this is a dilemma that will come up again and again, often several times a day. Just remember that the truth, as it exists in your reality, is likely to do more harm than good, and your objective should always be to find solutions that do no harm. You are a compassionate and wise person indeed if you can devise answers that satisfy both realities – yours and theirs.

When this happens, you have become an accomplished care partner and a true gift to your loved one. You have remembered that *We all deserve the best.*

Chapter Eight:
Compassion, Empathy,
and Self-interest

Let's discuss reality, how you -- as a care partner -- are responsible for it, and how you can manage it. No, I am not one of these people who says there is no reality except the one you create. Of course, there is. This book in your hand is part of your objective reality. But when it comes to your perceptions, emotions, and attitudes, your reality is far more flexible and manageable than you may think. And managing it is essential to effective dementia care.

Frustration and anger are feelings that all care partners experience. They are also toxic feelings that get in the way of being a good care partner. But what can you do about them? *He* made you angry! *He* won't do what you need him to do! To manage these feelings and hopefully convert them into positive and useful feelings, there are a couple of ideas you may want to consider.

First, bad behaviors toward you are not personal in the sense that they are thought out, strategic, and intentional. They are symptoms of the disease. Keep reminding yourself, "He is not trying to give me a hard time. He is having a hard time." This can be hard to accept in a relationship that has its own history of combat and disagreement, but you must accept the fact that taking behaviors personally will only impede your efforts to provide good care.

Second, you need to understand that you cannot replace a negative feeling with nothing. You cannot say, "I will no longer get angry." Under the circumstances, anger is a reasonable reaction, and if you just try to suppress it, pretty soon you will be angry at your own anger, and getting down on yourself is the last thing you need in these difficult moments.

A negative needs to be replaced with something else, preferably a positive. Let me suggest that you can replace anger with empathy. Try to stop focusing on your own feelings, focus on your loved one, and remind yourself again that he is having a hard time. Realize that his behaviors are acting out terrible feelings of fear and frustration. Empathize. I assure you, with deliberate effort and practice, this can become almost an automatic process. When confronted by bad behaviors, you can learn to bypass the anger and go right to empathy.

Frustration is another feeling that care partners frequently experience; perhaps several times a day. Again, try to step back from your own feelings and focus on the plight of your loved one. He is not willfully or maliciously doing the things that cause you such frustration. By altering your focus to the fact that he is having a very hard time, you can replace frustration with compassion, and with compassion comes patience.

Compassion and empathy are your greatest emotional tools in caring for someone with dementia. It will make things so much better for them, but what I want to suggest is that it will make things better for *you* we well. The negative feelings you are experiencing – though quite understandable – are arising from resentment and self-pity. By understanding and accepting this, you can turn self-pity into self-interest. And "self-interest" does not mean "selfishness."

Think about your own self-interest and ask, "Do I want to spend the rest of the day feeling this anger and allowing it to possibly lead me into bad judgments and unhelpful reactions?" "How long do I want to simmer in this frustration and feel resentful toward my loved one?" Understand that even if these feelings do not result in bad or neglectful care-giving, they certainly can be sensed by your loved one. Even if you don't act out these feelings, they can be sensed and turn your loved one's hard day into an even harder day.

Choose self-interest and give yourself a better day. Go through the logical processes that turn frustration to compassion and anger to empathy. You will find that your self-pity is replaced with a more self-confident and self-affirming feeling.

Yes, you have a hard job, and you probably didn't choose it, but it is in your own self-interest to make it as safe and manageable as you possibly can for both *you* and your loved one. If you allow yourself to remain swamped in bad feelings, it will continue to be bad for both of you.

Choose empathy, choose compassion, choose self-interest, and have a better day. And remember that *We all deserve the best.*

Chapter Nine:
When it's Show Time

Especially in the early stages of Alzheimer's or other forms of dementia, there is a surprising phenomenon that experienced care partners have seen many times, and we refer to it as "Show Time." Some people, especially in the early stages of dementia, have the ability to put on a convincing façade of normalcy for a short period of time, say ten or 15 minutes. It is an ability that can be quite exasperating for the care partner.

For example, you've been struggling with difficult behavior all day, especially with trying to get your loved one with dementia to get ready to see the doctor. It is always like this. He won't acknowledge your requests or instructions. He can't dress himself. He fiddles around while you are trying to get him to focus. It is almost as if he is deliberately trying to be late. Maybe so.

Then, you finally get in to see the doctor. You are absolutely frazzled, and you are sure that this time the doctor is finally going to understand how much your loved one has declined. But what does your loved one do? He's smiling, bright, chatty, utterly convincing that everything is just fine. You leave the doctor's office feeling angry and defeated. The doctor surely thinks *you* are the one with a problem. You've just experienced "Show Time!"

As long as people with dementia have the ability to "pull it together," this behavior is understandable. They know something is wrong, and the last thing they want is for people outside the family to realize it. They are embarrassed or ashamed of their condition, so they put on a happy face. As long as it does not require logic or complex thinking, it is possible to carry on small talk and answer the doctor's simple questions. "How do you feel?" "Fine." "Have you been sleeping?" "Yes." And they keep smiling.

"Show Time" can cause serious problems in families. Usually, based on living circumstances, one sibling will be in proximity to the parent with dementia and take on the task of providing care. Other siblings may be more than willing to help, but they live miles away. They may check in with you by phone, and they hear you describe all of the problems you are having.

Then, the parent with dementia gets on the phone for a few minutes, and it is show time again. Your brothers and sisters can't fathom what you are complaining about. Everything sounds fine to them. This can lead to serious disagreements about money, care practices, and family responsibilities. It's a problem that can irreparably damage families. You think that they think you have no credibility at all, and maybe they do.

Eventually -- and sadly -- your loved one will no longer be capable of "show time" behavior. But in the meantime, what can you do? I suggest you maintain a journal. I can see your jaw drop now. You're thinking, "With all of the exhausting stuff I have to put up with, you now want me to find time to start writing a book?" Yes, it is worth much more than the time you will put into it.

There are two types of journals. One is a log of the facts that lists behaviors and connects them to the time of day or the circumstances at the moment. Another is just jotting down your feelings. Don't try to psychoanalyze yourself. Just state how you feel. This one is for therapy. It will help you get the frustrations out of your mind and onto the paper. It will help you not relive them that night as you try to sleep after a difficult day.

The "factual" journal will come in handy when you are talking with your family, doctor, or counselor. In fact, your loved one probably would not have gotten away with "show time" with your doctor if you had such a journal to describe and document the time and place when specific problems arose. It will definitely convince a doctor to look beyond the superficial behavior.

I recommend doing both types of journaling. Write the log of events on the left-hand page, and later, on the right-hand page jot down how those events made you feel.

Trust me, such a journal will help you get through difficult times. Then, this too shall pass, and one day you will pick up your journal and realize what a really innovative, intelligent, and good person you are.

I also suggest that you attend local care partner support groups. Many of your peers will have experienced the same problems you have, and they can share ideals for solutions.

Until then, remember that *We all deserve the best!*

Chapter Ten:
Happier Holidays
for the Alzheimer's care partner

We have spoken before in this column about the kind of environment that facilitates better care for someone with Alzheimer's or dementia. You need a calm and quiet setting with low stimulation. You need stability and predictability so you can establish and stick to a routine. You need familiarity; not big surprises.

You will notice that we have just described an environment that is everything that the year-end holidays are NOT! The holidays break our routines; they introduce noise, lights, and loud music. They include parties, changes in diet, and social pressure to be in a jovial mood, whether we want to or not. Friends and relatives visit, or to meet our family obligations we must travel. All of this can be incredibly disruptive and even traumatic for someone living with dementia.

Rethinking holiday traditions
As a care partner approaching the holidays, you may need to resist or modify the "traditions" for the sake of your loved one and your own wellbeing. You need to confront the

fact that – at least in this difficult time of your life -- it is not your "job" to accommodate the demands of tradition and the expectations of your friends and relatives.

You can find ways to honor the traditions, but you may need to modify them to keep your care partner role as manageable as possible. You too deserve to have happy holidays, but you will need to plan, prepare, and make some changes to keep them as happy as possible, on your own terms. First and foremost, don't think for a minute that subjecting your loved one to all of the traditional activities is going to make them – or you – happy.

Avoid the hectic aspects of the season
Do not take your person with dementia shopping, or to parties, or to noisy and colorful events where there are crowds and loud music. If you have to do some of these things, get competent help to keep and care for your loved one at home for those hours you need to be away. If a neighbor, relative, or friend is not available, contact a professional companion service. These are not hard to find. They can provide an experienced senior person at a reasonable cost.

Some of these professional companions are retired nurses or care partners who understand your situation. Let me suggest that you plan ahead and not just "spring" outside or unfamiliar care on your loved one. Bring the person in for a couple of hours a time or two before you really need them. Let your loved one become familiar with them and allow them the opportunity to establish trust. They know how to do this; it is their job. It will cost you a little more, but it will be worth it when you return from a hectic day of shopping or visiting to find your loved one calm, happy, and comfortable in the care of their new "friend."

Your loved one may respond quite joyfully to the symbols of the season. For example, Christmas decorations or the symbolism of other religious holidays may be calming and reassuring for them. But you may need to tone it down a bit. For example, instead of hanging flashing bright lights on a tree, perhaps this year you use tiny white lights. Or perhaps you will want to play quieter music. Maybe you can have visitation from friends and relatives that your loved one is comfortable with, but these may need to be smaller, quieter, and for a shorter period of time.

Maybe there are some holiday activities that your loved one will enjoy and that will make them feel useful. Can they help put up decorations, with your supervision? Can they spend time making paper chains? They will appreciate the opportunity to help.

Be open and honest with friends and relatives about your needs
You should not hesitate to prepare visitors, whether they are friends or family. Write to them or have a conversation with them about the situation. Explain the dos and don'ts of contact with your loved one. Advise them not to rush in shouting and give a big hug. Explain they should approach your loved one gingerly with an outstretched hand and a lowered voice, allowing your loved one time to respond. Coach them that they should say something like, "Hello, Bill, it is so good to see you. I am your aunt Mary." They should not announce, "Hey, it's Mary. You remember me?" The word "remember" puts terrible pressure on someone with dementia. They are painfully aware that it is the core of their problem.

Prepping friends or relatives on how to behave can be a delicate situation, but you should not be embarrassed by it. If others can't empathize with your situation enough to modify their behavior, you're likely to not have a good outcome at any rate, so maybe they should not visit. Just remind yourself it is not your job to keep *their* holiday season "normal." It is your job to make it as happy and stress-free as you can for you and your loved one.

Don't force your loved one to 'get into' the season.

Don't force your loved one to dress up or change their eating habits for the occasion. Let them wear what they like and are comfortable in. If there is a dinner, don't serve them big helpings on unfamiliar china. Keep the routine; use their favorite plate. Serve their customary small helpings in courses rather than pile a plate to overflowing with things they may not recognize.

Adjust celebration activities to coincide with your loved one's best times of day. For example, don't start a meal or gathering in the late afternoon or evening when sun-downing may be setting in.

Through all of this, keep your expectations low. Do not expect family dynamics to change to accommodate your situation. If they do, great! But in most cases your family and friends can't begin to appreciate what you are dealing with. You can ask them to be patient with your loved one, but you must be fully prepared to be patient with them.

Turn to your friends and those who understand

I suggested above there may be ways to observe, but modify, your traditions. So, here's an idea: Why not host a holiday gathering for the members of your dementia support group? Make it a pot luck so you can reduce your preparatory time in the kitchen. Maybe some of them can bring their loved ones too. Or if not the whole group, limit it to those special people who mean the most to you. This could be a holiday gathering far more joyful and comfortable than any other.

The challenge of traveling

Traveling with your loved one should be avoided if possible, but in the real world you may feel that you have to. Taking your dementia person to a strange place can be especially stressful, and requires planning and preparation.

One of your first decisions may be whether you are driving or flying. Both will place you in environments that are constantly changing, unpredictable, and usually noisy.

Flying should be avoided

Flying is hectic and gives you less control than driving. Delays, noise, crowds, strange environments, and rushing to meet schedules will shatter any sense of routine. It is stressful enough for "normal" people, but it can be a frightening and confusing experience for your loved one, possibly leading to difficult or inappropriate behavior.

If you can take a non-stop flight – even at greater cost – you should do it. Most of the challenging circumstances of air travel take place in the terminals, so plane changes should be avoided.

Again, as with your friends and relatives, do not hesitate to explain your special circumstances. Ask for pre-boarding with adequate time to get your loved one settled in. Far forward may be preferable to sitting in the back watching all those strange people coming in, pushing and shoving and struggling with their luggage. Unless claustrophobia is an issue, place your loved one in the window seat where they won't be bumped and jostled during boarding. Give them a head set with music they like to help shut out the noise and confusion of other people boarding the plane. Advise the crew of your situation and coach them on how they might help.

If your loved one has to use the toilet, ask to use the lavatory in first class. This will avoid the long trek to the back of the airplane past rows of strangers.

Driving also has its challenges

If you hope to drive somewhere, you may want to take a short trial trip including one overnight stay to see how your loved one will react. Be aware that taking your loved one out of their routine and customary environment may cause difficult behavior and wandering. Someone who needs assistance with bathing, dressing, and toileting, or who is prone to paranoia or delusions will likely have real difficulty with traveling. If they cannot tolerate the short trial trip, you will surely not be successful on a longer trip.

This test can determine whether you should stay home, or ask family to come visit you instead. But if you feel you must travel, you may want to discuss it with your physician who may provide an anti-anxiety medication.
Again, use music to your advantage. I was lucky enough that I could put a headset on my husband Albert and he would sit quietly for hours, listing to music and watching the world go by.

Preparation can be the key

Being as prepared as possible will work in your

favor, whatever mode of travel you choose. Here are some pointers:

*Travel at your loved one's best time of day.
*Choose comfortable clothes and shoes.
*Allow time so you don't have to rush.
*At an airport, reserve a wheelchair or terminal taxi to limit the fatigue of walking.
*If flying, try to get a non-stop flight and inform the airline staff of your situation.
*If driving, stop frequently to hydrate, snack, and walk around. Stop early enough to have dinner and maintain the nightly routine.
*Have a bag packed with:

> *Drinks
> *Snacks
> *Activities and favorite items
> *Take your favorite music with headphones (to limit the noise and confusion)
> *Have emergency contact information
> *Have a list of current medications and dosages
> *Take copies of legal papers
> *Have a travel itinerary
> *Use an identification bracelet on your loved one and carry a current picture
> *Bring extra clothing
> *Bring incontinence products

Try to maintain a sense of humor, and enjoy your time as much as possible. Recognize when your loved one is showing signs of fatigue and agitation, and try to provide enough rest and quiet time. Remember to breathe and watch your stress level. The person you are with is taking cues from you. Be as flexible as possible and go with the flow. Have a back-up plan when possible.

Do it the way it works for you
In conclusion, planning and attitude are the key to having a holiday that is more enjoyable, safe, and as stress-free as possible. Being prepared can help avoid or better handle any mishaps that you encounter. Stay calm and ask for help from family and friends.

Remember that you are at a very important time in your life and dealing with difficult and unusual circumstances. Whenever you can, make things happen *your way*; which is not necessarily the way that traditions, family, and friends may expect of you.

You and your loved one come first, and remember that *We all deserve the best.*

Chapter 11:
Let's be positive about Alzheimer's

I can almost see you – the reader – doing a big double-take. "Positive about Alzheimer's? You must be crazy!"

I understand your reaction. It is the most feared disease in the world. There is no cure. And in the United States, diagnosis is growing at a rapid pace. What's there to be positive about?

First, as with other major diseases, the path to remediation or cure begins with public awareness. It is public awareness that eventually creates the political will that drives medical funding and a national desire to get serious about the problem.

This process began a little over 30 years ago when President Ronald Reagan declared – in 1983 – that November would be National Alzheimer's Disease Awareness Month. Ironically, a little more than 20 years later Reagan died of the very disease on which he had turned the national spotlight. Today, while funding for Alzheimer's research still lags behind other major diseases, there appears to finally be a positive momentum building. Congress has made significant increases in research funding, and the National Institute of Health has increased its commitment.

Since 1983, many state, regional, and national organizations have formed to improve public understanding and awareness of Alzheimer's disease. In 2017, a group of health care industry professionals in Citrus County became affiliated with Dementia Friendly America, a private sector non-profit organization devoted to education and awareness. My company, Coping with Dementia LLC, is one of the corporate sponsors of this project.

There are also in Citrus County more than 80 businesses and churches that have undergone training for certification as "Dementia Friendly." These have stepped up to provide service and support to people living with dementia and their care partners, and there is no doubt that more will join this movement.

Citrus County also has good private and public resources that include community centers, in-home services, care partner respite and relief programs, nutrition counseling, support groups, and more.

Research firms, located in nearby counties, are active in clinical trials to find causes and cures for dementia. These companies can provide free memory screening and offer opportunities for individuals to participate in their research, and get paid in the process. And in 2018, the nonprofit Dementia Education Inc. was created to develop programs and publications to support individuals living with dementia and their care partners. I am privileged to serve on the board of this organization, and I am especially excited about its long-term vision to create an institute for research, learning, and training in techniques of compassionate care.

In that regard, Teepa Snow, the highly-respected founder of the Positive Approach to Care, has spoken recently in Citrus County and venues in neighboring counties. Snow, one of the leading theoreticians, practitioners, and teachers of person-centered care in the United States, has developed new theories and a new body of techniques of care that utilize tone of voice, body language, appropriate touch, and rules of verbal interaction that bring more positive results to dementia care. Her methods reduce stress and conflict for both the care partner and the person with dementia.

I am a certified trainer in the Snow Methodology that focuses on the often-overlooked positive attributes of dementia care, rather than just struggling with the obvious negatives. While most researchers focus on the disease and a future cure, those of us practicing the Positive Approach to Care focus on the person, in the here-and-now. Until a cure is found, the most important thing we can do is preserve the quality of life for both the dementia person and their care partners.

Finally, while we are reviewing our "Alzheimer's assets," let's not overlook our local newspaper, the Citrus County Chronicle. We are fortunate to have a newspaper with an editorial leadership that has made a significant commitment to dementia education and awareness. Not only does the *Chronicle* frequently publish relevant news about dementia, it provides space for a monthly column that I am privileged to write.

So, I am serious when I say we should be positive about Alzheimer's and dementia. We can do this by focusing on our assets rather than our deficits. And until we meet again, please remember that W*e all deserve the best.*

Chapter 12:
Churches keep our loved ones social

At speaking engagements on Alzheimer's and dementia, I often stress the need to keep people living with dementia as sociable as possible in appropriate ways. Sociability may not change the course of the disease, but it will improve and enhance their quality of life.

What, you may ask, do I mean by "appropriate ways?" When I was an administrator at a memory care facility, I sometimes saw families take their loved one out for entertainment or events that resulted in disaster. The person with dementia returned rattled, angry, and confused, and sometimes physically aggressive. Too often, we subject our loved ones to what used to be fun for the family, such as a loud and busy restaurant. This is a level of stimulation they can no longer tolerate. To them, it is frightening and confusing and does not make for a happy time.

Rather, we must find ways for them to be with people that provides less visual and auditory stimulation. If we take our loved one out to eat, choose a bright and quiet restaurant, preferably early in the day. The evening hours can be more stressful due to the phenomenon known as sundowning, which can cause a person with dementia to become stressed, paranoid, and overly active. A low-light environment can do the same, so movies are not usually a good choice, especially the kind that feature explosions, violence, and mind-boggling special effects.

Admittedly, in our day-to-day life, social activities appropriate to someone living with dementia are not too easy to find. For this reason, many non-profit organizations involved in Alzheimer's and dementia have begun to sponsor Memory Cafes. These offer a unique experience apart from normal routines where people and their care partners meet in a quiet and supervised setting to pursue art and crafts, and sometimes music, in the company of others.

Churches can and do provide valuable service and social opportunities to people living with dementia and their families. First of all, church attendees in America represent a relevant demographic. Depending on the denomination, their membership over the age of 50 can range from 49 to 55 percent of the congregation. This is the age group that either has some level of dementia, or is caring for a parent or loved one with dementia.

A great many of our churches and denominations build their missions around service to the community, both within their membership and for the outside community at large. They often have enthusiastic and dedicated committees of volunteers whose job is to fulfill that mission of service. And, as non-profit organizations, they often do fund-raising dedicated to programs and causes for the betterment of their communities.

The importance of churches in providing service to people with dementia has been recognized in European countries to the extent that their socialized medical systems provide funding for faith-based programs for care, outreach, and support for people living with dementia. Guides and "tool kits" have been developed to provide guidance in setting up events and programs that help keep individuals with dementia active and social.

Here in the United States, we do not have such a funding source, but this has not stood in the way of churches getting involved in building programs to help people with dementia. Here in Citrus County, a full 20 percent of our churches have sponsored training to become certified "dementia friendly."

To be certified Dementia Friendly, churches need to sponsor a workshop attended by at least 15 to 20 of their members. These workshops are offered by Coping with Dementia LLC and can be conducted for congregation members only, or opened to the public at large. They last about two hours, and they are free.

In addition, the Citrus-based nonprofit Dementia Education Inc. has created a handbook for dementia friendly congregations. It too is free. Contact me at deb@oping.today for more information about the workshops of the handbook.

And until next month, please remember that *We all deserve the best.*

Chapter 13:
The third person

Most people caring for their loved one living with dementia feel a strong obligation to provide the best care possible. This is good, but not when they believe they are the *only one* who can provide that care. Perhaps they are among the minority who still stigmatize the disease and want no one outside the household to know what is happening. Or perhaps they feel that no one else understands and loves their dementia person as much as they do.

These, or any other excuses to be a sole care partner are wrong. They will lead to pain, suffering, and exhaustion, and possibly a *poorer* quality of care than you intended to provide. This month I want to talk about the importance of a third person, for the benefit of both you and your loved one.

Many times, I have seen a care partner's health decline from the overwhelming task of caring for a person with dementia 24/7. With an intense focus on the care of their loved one, they often ignore their own health and feelings, or rationalize that it will eventually be over and then they can get back to normal. This disease can last a long time, and sadly, the stress of caring can sometimes take the care partner first, which is the worst possible result for both parties.

This "third person" can actually be many people helping you from time to time. It may be a friend, neighbor, church member, family member, or even someone from a companion service. Avoiding care partner burnout may require a team to perform different tasks, such as taking out the garbage, seeing that the lawn is tended to, picking up groceries, cooking meals, or just sitting with your loved one. Individually, these tasks may seem incidental, but every moment that you can clear your mind, rest, and tend to yourself is solid gold.

Acceptance of help with your caring task should come sooner rather than later. Get your loved one familiar and comfortable with your helpers. When a person with dementia accepts having someone else in their home, the relationship will be more comfortable and natural as they inevitably decline.

But I also want to talk about the importance of a special third person – an individual who has the understanding, skill, and compassion to provide emotional support and assist with tasks beyond the incidental. Hopefully, you have access to a friend or relative who has experienced this disease; who really understands what you are going through. We have talked before about the importance of attending a support group. Perhaps your support group leader will know someone who has already traveled this path.

This special third person may be able to more effectively communicate with your loved one than you can. This is not because you are a bad care partner, but because they have a different perspective that is not influenced by the "family dynamic," the learned and ingrained behaviors we all have that may shortcut or confuse good communication.

This is a concept that many care partners are not open to. "How can anyone provide better care than I can, because I know my loved one better than anyone else does." We must learn that with the progress of the disease, the "normal" time-tested relationship may cease to work. As the person with dementia changes, the care partner must change as well. This is not easy! The old ways with which we got results – our speech patterns, vocabulary, body language -- no longer work. The care partner – in the throes of this change – is usually the last to understand why. This is when a special third person can help.

Accept the fact that your journey is not a "sprint" but a "marathon." Actually, maybe we should think of it as a "marathon relay" where it is necessary to pass off the baton of responsibility from time to time in order to be successful. To be the best care partner you can, you need to become open to the idea of the third person, whether this is a special person or a team. Better still if you have both.

Accept help! You owe it to yourself, and when you take care of yourself you can take better care of your loved one.

And keep in mind that *We all deserve the best!*

Chapter 14:
Keeping the Love

This month is all about love. Valentine's day is when we give and receive flowers, chocolate, gifts, and cards that show that we are loved and cared for by someone else. For many, it is a happy time to reflect on memories of love, friends, and family.

For those caring for a loved one with dementia, this season can be a bitter reminder of what we have lost. It can remind us how cruel this disease really is; not just a taker of health but also a taker of joy.

Recently, a care partner in a support group I facilitate asked, "What happens if you fall out of love with your person with dementia?" I had never heard this question before, and I was taken aback. I suspect that many care partners have felt this way during their journey, but hearing one openly express this pain surprised me. I had to pause and take a deep breath.

After a moment, I said, "You have allowed the dementia to come between you and the person you love. In its endless demands and challenges, dementia has taken center stage in your life so that you can no longer see the one you love. You must try to bring the name and identity of your loved one back to the fore." I thought of something Teepa Snow says: "They are who they were, but they have changed."

Refocusing on your loved one – rather than the disease – is not easy to do. Your person living with dementia may look the same, but they have become different. Their problems and behaviors have brought many "un-loving" moments and feelings into your life.

This is the time to call upon compassion; to remember he (she) is not intentionally making your life miserable. He is not deliberately giving you a hard time; he is having a hard time. If he had the choices that we rational people of sound mind enjoy, he would never do this on purpose. Remind yourself of this, and try to look beyond the disease to see that the person is still here. Though they have changed, inside they are still who they were.

Let me offer a few tips on how to rekindle the love. Spend some time reminiscing over old photographs about where and when you met, what the first thing was that attracted you to each other. Study those sweet smiles and bright eyes. Try to avoid using the word "remember;" just ask your loved one if he would like to talk about what he sees in these pictures.

He is likely to remember more about these long-ago occasions than something that happened just yesterday. Individuals with Alzheimer's or dementia may feel lost and confused in the present, but in the memories of the past they may find peace and joy. You may see your loved one perk up, start to talk, smile, and laugh about the things that may have happened. You may even for just a brief moment have your person back with you, remembering very clear and vivid memories that perhaps you have forgotten.

If they get it wrong; if what they see is really not what happened, do not correct them. It is *their* reality and memories, flawed though they may be. Get into their reality and let them talk about history as they remember it. Validate what they have to say. Facts are of no importance; feelings are. It is in these human feelings you will regain the ability to look beyond the disease to see, enjoy, and love the person.

Or, you may want to listen to your loved one's favorite music. Maybe ask them to dance or sing with you. Music has remarkable healing powers and can restore joy and resurrect good memories that may have been long gone. It takes us into places and times that were fulfilling and comforting. I have seen people correctly sing multiple verses of a song, even after they can no longer put together a rational sentence.

If you have the ability to do so, take your loved one to visit a place of fond memories; maybe a park or landmark or one of the favorite places you went on dates. Or celebrate days that have special meaning for the two of you, even if your loved one cannot respond with as much joy and recognition as you would like them to. Keep reminding yourself that they are trying.

Through photos, music, and reminiscence, you may get that person you loved to shine through – perhaps for just a moment. But that moment can be enough to look beyond the disease and into the person that still deserves your love and compassion.

Realizing that Alzheimer's comes with good and bad days, keep your expectation low. If it works out, then it is a good day; it is a "Valentine's Day." If your loved one is having a bad day and it does not work out, do not try to force them to remember. Even if these techniques of connection do not bring joy to your loved one, maybe they will for you. Remember that caring for a person with dementia requires caring for yourself as well.

Try to use this year's Valentine's Day as a day of reminiscence and recovery, not a day to grieve what you have lost. Behind the disease, the one you loved is still there.

And don't forget that *we all deserve the best.*

Chapter 15:
Practicing Compassionate Care can get better results

To paraphrased the American poet Maya Angelou: "People will forget what you said, people will forget what you did, but people will not forget how you made them feel."

I think this wise observation is true for all of us, including those who are living with dementia. We can overlook many of the things that affect us intellectually, but it is harder to overlook those things that have impacted us emotionally, in our hearts and souls.

We know that with dementia the loss of memory is the most obvious symptom. First, there is loss of short-term memory – what we did or ate yesterday. This progresses to loss of longer-term memories until it appears that a person in latter stages of dementia remembers nothing.

This loss is so discouraging and dramatic, it is easy for us to conclude that a person with dementia has lost every aspect of themselves. But my experience tells me this is not entirely true. They will lose their recollection of events and things, but I know they do not lose their feelings; their *emotional memory*.

To the contrary, I think as cognition declines, their feelings may become heightened, or more important to them. This means that how we treat them really matters. Dismissive attitudes and harsh words are hurtful, and I believe people with dementia can feel this hurt.

Do not conclude that these feelings do not exist just because the person with dementia cannot tell you about them with words. They have other ways of telling you. For example, withdrawing or striking out may be a direct response to how you have made them feel. They don't like it and they are telling you the only way they can.

To avoid these conflicts, I urge students, clients, and care partners to practice compassionate care. What does this mean? The word "compassion" literally means "suffering together." It is not sympathy, it is not pity. With sympathy or pity you still stand apart as an observer of the other person. You may be sympathetic toward them, but you are not suffering with them.

But how can we step into their suffering, and why should we? Am I saying that to be a good care partner we have to be as miserable and unhappy and helpless and confused as they are? Certainly not.

First, we need to step back and consider what happens to a relationship as a person slips into dementia. Their reality changes, a little at first but finally it changes radically. Their vision changes, their ability to understand conversation at a normal rate disappears. Their small motor skills, especially with tasks like buttoning buttons or tying shoes, degrade. They begin to experience neuropathy; tingling or numbness in their hands and feet. While they still have the power of speech, they experience extreme anxiety and frustration because they cannot remember a common and frequently used word. They can't tell you what they want, which can lead to anger and impatience.

In short, their reality has radically changed while yours has not. For them this is real, and you cannot reason or argue them out of it, no matter how hard you try. The most painful and dysfunctional relationships between care partners and their loved ones with dementia are actually the result of a battle between realities. Ending this battle is your responsibility, not theirs.

There is no point in trying to drag them back into your reality, and the more you try will only result in an ever more stressful and dysfunctional relationship. You cannot expect them to change, so you must be the one to change if you really want to reduce the pain, suffering, and frustration in your care-giving tasks and responsibilities.

When I speak about compassion as "suffering together," what I am talking about is doing your very best to understand and accept their reality. Of course, you cannot do this in a literal sense; you cannot really know what they are thinking or feeling all the time. But just accepting the fact that their reality is different and every bit as legitimate for them as yours is for you is a huge step toward the practice of compassionate care.

It is a challenging task that your own sense of reality will struggle against every day. But I promise you that the rewards are rich. Being a care partner will become less conflicted and less stressful. Those times that the relationship clicks, and you know that you have just made things easier for your loved one are extremely rewarding.

Through this effort to "suffer together" through an acceptance and better understanding of their reality, you both will suffer less. Again, to paraphrase Maya Angelou, "They may not remember what you said or did, but they will certainly remember how you make them feel." And good feelings are the bedrock of a better quality of life, even for those living with dementia.

And remember -- *We all deserve the best!*

Chapter 16:
Why we should have
a conversation about driving

During my speaking engagements, I often hear questions about driving; questions like "When is it time to take away the keys?" Understandably, people want to avoid this decision as long as possible, and often they let impaired loved ones continue to drive with rationalizations like, "They do just fine when I am with them." "He only drives the car locally." "She hasn't had an accident yet."

Taking away driving privileges from someone with dementia is one of the toughest decisions you will face. Driving represents independence, freedom, even a reason for being. For some, taking away their ability to drive can amount to taking away their reason for living.

One of the changes in a person with dementia is the loss of peripheral vision and depth perception. In some cases, these changes can take place early-on in the course of the disease. The loss of peripheral vision can eliminate their ability to see or recognize a traffic sign on the side of the road, or to see a pedestrian who has already stepped off the curb, or to realized they are already being overtaken by a car in a lane they intend to turn into.

Loss of depth perception can lead to driving over parking bumper, not realizing how close you are to the car stopped ahead of you, or not comprehending the approaching speed of another car coming from the right or left at an intersection.

Most of us do not realize just how much we drive with our "ears." Hearing is an important factor in knowing that someone is in the lane next to you, or picking up quickly on the fact that an emergency vehicle is in the area. The driver with dementia likely has impaired hearing, exacerbating the problems already caused by impaired vision.

To these sensory deficiencies, add the fact that dementia results in a lack of judgment, decision making ability, and increased reaction time. In addition, a person with dementia loses the ability to comprehend spatial relationships and recognize landmarks. This can lead to getting lost, and getting lost in a car is a problem. There are many stories of individuals who drove until they ran out of gas, ending up hundreds of miles from home.

Letting a person with dementia continue to drive can result in much worse than an occasional fender bender. If this person already has a diagnosis, their legal liability will be increased. Even using meds that are associated with Alzheimer's – even in the absence of a diagnosis – can give a plaintiff's attorney a lot of ammunition. The result could be more than the loss of one's driving license. It could be the loss of every material asset your family owns!

But how do we face this awful decision to take away a love one's driving privilege? One thing you can try is to engineer a transition to the passenger seat. Offer to drive while your loved one enjoys the scenery. Ask a friend to come by to take your loved one to lunch or coffee, which will provide another opportunity for them to get accustomed to being a passenger.

When driving your loved one, tell them how much you enjoy their being with you. Make them feel useful and appreciated. This will maintain their dignity and help them understand that not driving is NOT a punishment.

You may need to place the car out of sight and out of mind. In this case, you might tell them it is in the shop. You may feel bad about this because you feel you are "lying," but you must keep in mind that their safety is the overriding concern.

I've even heard of people who replaced their family car with a new model that had a push-button starter and screen display digital instrumentation. The "cockpit" was so alien that the person with dementia did not mind moving to the passenger seat.

At one workshop, a woman told me a solution that is incredibly novel. For years, her husband had walked out the back door and climbed behind the steering wheel. She backed the car into the driveway, and the next time he climbed in, he was in the passenger seat. Believe it or not, it worked! She got in and drove and he said nothing about it. He never drove again.

But this happy solution reveals a very scary situation. Just how long had this man been driving on "auto pilot," so oblivious that when a change came, he did not even miss the steering wheel? Think about that. Driving is an ingrained behavior, and your loved one may already be far more impaired and dangerous than you realize.

You may need to get some help with taking

away the keys. If you have a good relationship with your physician, you can ask that she (he) recommend that your loved one stop driving. In some states, there is an online form available from the Division of Motor Vehicles (DVM) that has a place for your physician's signature. This signature is not required, but it is a way to involve a third party, which can reduce stress for the family.

Taking away the keys is a difficult and emotional decision. But you must remember that the safety of your person with dementia and the safety of others is paramount.

And remember that *"We All Deserve the Best."*

Chapter 17:
Planning will head off problems

I am sure someone will say, "It has never happened to me," "I will not have to evacuate," or "I know where everything is." All this may be true, but when you are caring for someone who may not be competent to assist with an evacuation, you must be prepared and ready prior to the emergency, whatever that emergency may be.

In Florida, we think of hurricanes as the most likely cause for evacuation, but this may not be the only emergency we must be prepared for. Anything that will remove you from your place of safety, routine, and comfort can be an emergency to a person living with Alzheimer's and other forms of dementia.

When you are stressed and overwhelmed, so is your person with dementia. They will feed off your emotions. This is why being prepared is so important; so that when it happens you can focus on your loved one, and not what you may have forgotten.

Here are some of the things you should take care of prior to an emergency:

*   If staying with family or a friend during evacuation is an option, be sure this is agreed upon and prepared for in advance.
*   If a shelter is the only option, call your local county services to register in a special needs shelter (they normally open these shelters early).
*   Wherever you plan to evacuate, don't wait until the last minute. The longer you wait, the more hectic the situation may become.
*   You should take copies of all legal paperwork with you, such as medical information, power of attorney, insurance papers, and a list of emergency contacts (physician, family, etc.). I know care partners who keep such documents in the glove box of their car, which is a good idea.
*   Have a three-day supply of medications and don't forget to update the medications in the kit when prescriptions are changed.
*   Have three days of clothes (easy on and off). To reduce confusion for your loved one, the clothes should be comfortable and familiar to them.
*   Have incontinence supplies, if needed.
*   If they wear eyeglasses, get a spare pair for the kit.
*   If they require oxygen, take a spare tank.

*Bottled water and even some of their favorite snacks and drinks should be included.

* Have a current picture with name, address, and other important information written on the back.

* Flashlights, radio, and batteries should be included.

* Take a spare cell phone charter.

* Necessary toiletry items, and include hand cream which can be used to sooth and calm a person.

* Simple pastime activities such as cards, puzzles, board games, and books (coloring).

* Have some kind of ID on your loved one, such as a bracelet.

* Think about a Human Scent Preservation Kit with your loved one's pure scent, because in an unfamiliar place and out of their normal routine they may tend to wander away, seeking their home.

* You may find that some type of head phone or iPod with your loved one's favor music will bring them comfort.

* Make sure they have a place to lie down and rest or nap when needed.

* If they have a favorite item, such as a blanket or pillow, be sure to take it with you.

* If your person is a resident in a care community, ask about their disaster and evacuation plans.

This may sound like very tall order to most care partners, but preplanning for unexpected events is the best thing you can do for both of you. You may want to consider doing this at a time when your person is not present to avoid creating unnecessary anxiety. Then put your kit somewhere for safe keeping.

Preparing a kit now will give you time to think through your needs when you are not under pressure. I promise, if you try to collect what you need under the pressure of an imminent evacuation or emergency, you will certainly forget important items.

Removing your loved one from home in an emergency may distress them, possibly causing behavior issues that you have not experienced before. This is when you have to stay as calm as possible, hold hands, speak calmly, validate and reassure that you are with them and will not let them out of your sight. Re-direct their concerns, try to avoid noisy places, validate their feelings, and remind them you are there for them.

Being prepared is the best way to turn an emergency into a manageable situation.

And remember my slogan: "We all deserve the best."

Chapter 18:
Validation Therapy

Our natural reaction is to correct a person with dementia when they say something that is not factual or historically correct. This is what we do with children. When they say something wrong, we immediately correct them because this is how they learn. This works because, unlike a person with dementia, a normal child does not have cognitive impairment.

But a person with dementia is not a child who is still in the learning phase of life. They have a disease that plays havoc with their ability to remember and reason. Correcting their mistakes is not useful for two reasons. First, they are no longer able to learn. And second, it only frustrates, humiliates, or embarrasses them to be told they are wrong. Yes, people with dementia have *feelings*. It is a quality of the mind they do not lose.

I encourage care partners to use "validation therapy," which is the practice of responding positively to the dementia person's ideas and beliefs, even if you believe (or know) they are *wrong* within the context of your own reality.

This empathetic approach to dementia care was developed by Naomi Feil and described in her book "The Validation Breakthrough: Simple Techniques for Communicating with People with Alzheimer's type Dementia," published in 2002. It is based on the idea that remarks and beliefs of people with dementia should be treated with respect as a legitimate expression of their feelings; not dismissed, or disputed because those ideas wrong or not factual. To state this methodology very simply, in a way we have all heard before, the validation method of care is to "walk in the dementia person's shoes."

Let's look at some examples:

You notice that your mother with dementia is pacing and anxious, and you invite her out for some ice cream. This usually works, but this time your mother says, "I can't go now. I am waiting for my mother, and she is late." This is when a care partner may become frustrated because they have faced this issue many times before, and reply, "Stop it! You know your mother is not coming. She is dead!"

Wrong! Very wrong! This is cruel because your loved one really does not know that her mother is dead. She is living in a different reality that is just as valid for her as your reality is for you. Your job is to respect and validate her beliefs. Otherwise, you will only increase her stress and perhaps even turn it into anger when she looks back at you in pain and despair and says, "When? Why didn't you tell me?"

One approach is to say something like, "It's okay. We have plenty of time to get some ice cream before she comes by." Some care partners react very strongly to this because it is a "lie." It violates their own moral values and need to be honest. Others, who may have more experience in validation therapy, will see it not as a lie, but as a validation of the dementia person's reality.

But let me suggest another way that skirts the issue of whether her mother is alive. You can say something like, "I know you love and have had some wonderful times with your mother. Can you tell me about her?" This will take the dementia person out of the moment and enable them to reminisce and hopefully get beyond their current state of anxiety. Generally, just saying "Tell me about it" can be a very useful tool. It allows the person with dementia to express their feelings, which is really what they want and need to do.

When I managed a memory care facility, one day I noticed one of our residents pacing back and forth in the hallway, and mumbling, clearly in a state of anxiety. I approached and asked what was going on. He answered, "Got to plant the corn!" I knew he had been a farmer his whole life and that missing planting time was something he could not allow.

I replied "Oh, I did not realize it is already that time. I have the supplies in the shed. I will go get them so that we can get started." I asked for acknowledgement, got it, and off I went. By the time I walked the building and came back to him he had calmed down and was sitting in the lunch room having a snack.

We need to understand that for a person with dementia, anxiety is like a hamster in a wheel, spinning around and around. Those of us without dementia can "think" or "talk" ourselves out of this state. They cannot. They need an outside intervention that will kick that hamster out of the wheel and allow them to settle down.

And believe me, challenging, disputing, or belittling their "incorrect" beliefs is not the intervention they need. This can only make the hamster go faster, plus make it angry. What they need is an empathetic, compassionate intervention that will validate their feelings. Then they will settle down and move on to their next moment. For our farmer friend, it was a snack. Hunger, which he might have interpreted as missing planting time, may have been what he was feeling all along.

If, through validation, you can reduce stress and anxiety in your loved one, you will reduce stress and anxiety in yourself. This is preferable to a pointless battle of realities that never resolves anything. You don't need to argue about facts. You only need to validate feelings. You may find yourself rewarded in many ways that you did not expect.

Until next time, let's remember that *We all deserve the best!*

Chapter 19:
Getting lost; It only takes one time

Many thoughts have run through my mind since the alert went out last week about a person with memory issues who went missing. Events like this are tragic, traumatic for families, and disruptive to entire communities. Witness the enormous effort by law enforcement agencies and volunteers that has gone into the search for her!

This case has hit us hard in Citrus County, but it is a situation that happens far more frequently than many people realize. More than 60 percent of people with Alzheimer's or another form of dementia will wander, and if a person is not found within 24 hours, the odds are that the wanderer will suffer serious injury or death.

In my work, I have provided many hours of education to care partners about the danger and likelihood of wandering, but too many seem to take false comfort in the belief that "It won't happen to me." So often I hear responses like, "Well, he hasn't wandered yet," "He never leaves my sight," or "It won't happen because all he does is sit in his chair."

I do not know whether people are really this unconvinced, or whether it is such a frightening prospect that they immediately leap into a state of denial. But for whatever the reason, it seems to be a topic that we too often dismiss lightly . . . until it is too late.

In my workshops and support groups, I tell a story about my son who owns a swimming pool. Some years ago, even before his young son could walk, he began to install a safety fence around the pool. They did not wait for their child to become a toddler, and they did not wait for him to fall into the pool for the first time before they took preventive measures. Yet it seems so much harder for us to anticipate this kind of potential tragedy when there is an adult with dementia involved, rather than a child.

You might say, "Well this was their responsibility as parents. The real and present danger is obvious!" To this I would respond that when we know six out of ten adults with dementia will wander, the real and present danger should be equally obvious. Just as with the likelihood of the child drowning, we need to put countermeasures in place as soon as the problem becomes imaginable.

One of the most important things we can do is get a human scent preservation kit, commonly called a Scent Kit. They are readily available in Citrus County; from the Sheriff's Office, from Find M-Friends, from my company Coping with Dementia, from the libraries, and from the community centers. These kits enable scent-discriminating dogs to rapidly find or lead first responders to a person who has gone missing.

I should add here that scent kits are equally important for children, especially those with autism or mental disability. I urge everyone to get a scent kit now, before you need it, rather than later, in which case it could be too late.

I have observed also that it is difficult for care partners to make that 911 call when a loved one has gone missing. Perhaps they are embarrassed, or perhaps they underestimate the seriousness of the situation. They may wait for hours, hoping their person will turn up, or that they will find them without outside help. Don't delay! If you cannot find your person in 30 minutes, you may have already waited too long. Get on the phone and call for help.

I too went through this with my husband Albert. As his disease progressed, he began to leave the house while I was at work. More than once a neighbor or a Sheriff's deputy called me to say they had found him and were bringing him home. This was because he had a wanderer's ID bracelet with my phone number on it.

But each time this happened, he was able to get farther away from home. It is shocking how far a person can travel in a short time. And wanderers with dementia do not have a plan. They are simply wandering, and usually, they will travel "down terrain" simply because gravity makes it easier to do so. Eventually, traveling down-terrain is likely to lead to water, a lake, a retention basin, a wetland.

Now I look back and realize I was one of the lucky ones, and my message to others is that it is foolish to rely on luck. Please do not take the hazard of wandering lightly. There are important things you can do to avoid tragedy. More countermeasures than we have space to discuss here are available. I refer you to the Alzheimer's Association website: http://www.alz.org/care/alzheimers-dementia-wandering.asp#who

Chapter 20:
Citrus County
ahead for Dementia Safety

Previously, I have written about the Citrus County program to distribute Scent Kits to help first responders more quickly find individuals with dementia who have wandered and gone missing. To date, more than 5,000 kits have been distributed throughout the county. This is a big accomplishment for which we can credit mainly the non-profit Find M-Friends and our Sheriff's Office.

Find M-Friends also trains and provides the bloodhounds that first responders use to find missing persons, which may include children as well as individuals living with dementia. It is a vital service that many police agencies have not yet incorporated into their K-9 divisions.

I am even more excited to tell you about a new program from our Sheriff's Office that puts Citrus County on the leading edge of Florida communities seeking to keep our citizens safe; especially those with dementia. It is a voluntary and confidential registration program that allows care partners of persons with dementia– and also parents of those with autism – to submit information to the department's records system that will provide vital and more complete data to responding deputies, providing a tool to help them do their work more rapidly and more responsively to specific situations.

Under this program, care partners can place on file specific information about their loved one, including whether or not they have a Scent Kit that can speed up the process of search and rescue. In the event of a 911 call, this information can be accessed by a dispatcher and provided to deputies who are able to respond with knowledge that can speed their work, guide their approach, and head off potential conflicts.

It is a program that can improve the safety of a person or family in crisis, as well as the safety of the officers on the scene. But what excites me most is the fact that this special information system database can potentially reduce the number of Baker Acts of individuals living with Alzheimer's and dementia. I have always maintained that the Baker Act is a blunt and inappropriate tool to use on people with dementia, and the less it is required, the better.

Using the program is easy. Those of you caring for individuals living with dementia (or autism), can register your loved one's confidential and vital information online. Just go to the Citrus County Sheriff's official web site (www.sheriffcitrus.org).

Toward the right of the screen you will find a button that says "How do I?" This will click into a drop-down menu that includes "Register someone with Autism/Dementia." It's as easy as that. Your information is protected under Florida public records laws and the Health Insurance Portability and Accountability Act (HIPAA).

If you ever have to call for help, responding officers will arrive on the scene already in possession of useful information to help them do their job more efficiently in keeping you and your loved one safe. This, combined with our county scent kit program, makes our county even more Dementia Smart and Dementia Friendly. Our thanks to all concerned with this visionary and vital program.

It is consistent with my moto: *We all deserve the best.*

Chapter 21:
Ten reasons for early screening and diagnosis

People have asked me, "Why should I get a memory screening for Alzheimer's? If it is irreversible and incurable, why bother to get a diagnosis?"

The best reason for early screening and diagnosis is to learn that you *don't* have dementia. There are correctable medical conditions that create symptoms similar to dementia. Under these circumstances, you may be showing signs of dementia, which you don't actually have.

When people have **degraded hearing**, they sometimes adopt behaviors similar to a person with dementia. This may include social and conversational withdrawal, a catatonic gaze, or tentative physical movement. All of us, as we age, should have our hearing tested. Your condition may be easily correctable.

Normal Pressure Hydrocephalus is a buildup of spinal fluid in the brain, and it can cause "Alzheimer's gait," loss of balance, and memory problems. It is a serious condition, but it can be corrected with surgery.

Binge drinking and heavy alcohol use can result in dementia. It is a double-edged sword. Alcohol can destroy brain cells, but heavy use can also lead to poor dietary practices that result in thiamine (Vitamin B-1) deficiency. This can result in Wernicke-Korsakoff Syndrome which causes memory loss, confusion, and hostile behavior. But WKS is treatable. It is not an irreversible dementia.

Over-medication can cause dementia-like symptoms. Sad to say, but sometimes doctors prescribe drugs on drugs, seeking to mask specific symptoms without adequate consideration for the effect of drug combinations. If you are taking "a lot" of different drugs, ask your doctor to review your whole regimen, or seek a second opinion. Look up the Beers Criteria on the internet. It is a list of drugs that should be used with caution or not at all by older people.

Diabetes can contribute to irreversible dementia because too much or too little glucose can damage blood vessels in the brain. It is important to detect diabetes early and manage it faithfully. It does not have to lead to dementia.

Depression can affect memory, mood, reasoning, and behavior. A psychiatrist or neurologist is qualified to determine whether your problem is depression or dementia. Mood altering medication and lifestyle changes can be prescribed to deal with depression.

Vitamin B-12 deficiency can also result in dementia-like behavior. Such deficiency can be corrected with medication taken orally or by injection.

One of the most common, and often overlooked causes of "false dementia" is a **Urinary Tract Infection**. UTIs, especially in seniors, can lead to dizziness, confusion, delirium, and hallucinations. Good hygiene can help avoid UTIs, and antibiotics, rest, and lots of liquids – specifically Cranberry juice – can cure them.

Thyroid imbalance – either too little or too much – can cause dementia-like symptoms. This can be determined with a simple blood test, and corrected with medication and sometimes surgery.

Even if you are not experiencing symptoms of dementia, it is a good idea to get a screening to establish a medical baseline from which any future decline in memory can be measured. We establish baselines for breast cancer, even when we have no reason to believe we have it. We establish baselines for bone density that will help us identify problems at a later date. Why not take the same precautions toward dementia?

So, these are ten good reasons for early screening and diagnosis. Many research companies involved in the study of Alzheimer's will give you a screening at no charge. Because it is their business, these screenings will be a far more thorough process than you will receive from most general practitioners. Even if your doctor is not an expert in dementia, you will be helping him or her by submitting a dementia screening report to your medical file.

A neurologist or psychiatrist is qualified to diagnose Alzheimer's and other causes of dementia, but again, you may be able to facilitate this process by providing them your memory screening report.

Finally, let me reiterate that if you have the slightest concern about whether you or a loved one are developing memory problems or other symptoms of dementia, *do not* remain in a state of fear and uncertainty. Early diagnosis may very well determine that you have dementia-like symptoms that are correctable.

This can bring relief to you and your own family.

You should take precautionary steps early *because We all deserve the best.*

Chapter Twenty-Two:
What is "Sundowning?"

Sundowning is a term used to describe a phenomenon that affects more than half of people who are in mid to late stages of dementia. It gets its name from the time of day when it is most prevalent.

In the afternoon or toward evening, many people living with dementia become more distressed, obsessive, agitated, and less easily re-directed away from their anxiety. This personality change may be severe enough to include delusions and even hallucinations. It may include more persistence pacing and exit seeking. It creates a higher risk of elopement, and it may become more difficult to get your loved one to eat, hydrate, and even sleep.

Obviously, Sundowning makes the task of care much more difficult, and heightened frustration, anxiety, and anger for the care partner only contribute to bad experiences and potentially bad results. During Sundowning, there is a greater chance for abuse and neglect. So, it is very important to understand and recognize the phenomenon, and have a plan and the caring tools to deal with it, or even head it off.

There are a number of theories about what causes Sundowning, including some pretty complicated ideas about the disruption of *circadian rhythms* causing chemical changes in the brain. For me, it is explanation enough to understand that your loved one is simply exhausted from trying to get through the day.

A person living with dementia is experiencing sensory disruption and confusion at a level many of us simply cannot understand. The daily events that glide by largely unnoticed by most of us can be overwhelmingly confusing and unmanageable for a person with dementia. Little wonder that by late afternoon or early evening they are simply worn out, frazzled, and beyond the limits of their diminished ability to cope.

As a care partner, you need to first learn to recognize the signs of Sundowning because – contrary to its name – it can happen at other times of day as well, though in most cases it happens in the afternoon or evening. Keep a journal, and note when you see the increased anxiety and the exaggerated behaviors described above. This will help you identify when Sundowning may begin for your person, which will dictate when you need to take pre-emptive action.

Get your loved one to rest prior to his or her Sundowning time. This can head off the exhaustion that can send your loved one into an emotional crisis.

Discourage visitors during the hour prior to the time you expect Sundowning to begin. This is necessary to promote rest and reduce stimulation.

Reduce noise stimulation, such as the radio or television. Even in circumstances that do not include Sundowning, we must be careful about the use of these devices. Avoid news or any kind of loud or violent programming. Avoid loud music. Play soft or soothing music.

Many people with dementia love one or two specific movies; often they are musicals. It does not matter how many times the person with dementia watches these favorites; they continue to enjoy them. These can be used to put your person into a quieter, more tranquil state of mind prior to the period when Sundowning may begin.

Pay attention to the level of lighting. If Sundowning is expected in the late afternoon or evening, increase the interior lighting and draw the shades. As it becomes dark outside, your loved one will see their reflection in windows. They may not recognize this as their reflection. For a person with dementia, these reflections will become frightening strangers invading their home and their lives.

Try not to schedule appointments or travel outside the home in the afternoon. Any daily tasks that are difficult for your person should be scheduled in the morning, whenever possible.

As a general rule of care, learn, note, and adhere to the schedule of activities that seem less challenging for your loved one. Create and try to stick to a daily routine, whether or not Sundowning is involved.

Limit caffeine and sugars to the morning.

Learn what can be "beneficial distractions," such as photo albums, fidget mats, dolls, or stuffed animals that your loved one seems to enjoy.

Without contributing to exhaustion, give your person simple but useful things to do, such as folding towels. This gives them a task to focus on which may distract them from the environmental changes going on around them.

Make sure they are comfortable; that their clothes are dry, that they are not hungry or thirsty, and that they are not too hot or cold.

Validate their feelings. Never argue with them or tell them their perceptions are wrong or non-existent. I know of a case when a person was upset about children playing in the corner of her room. This was clearly a hallucination, but the care partner simply told the children they had to leave and made a conspicuous motion of shooing them out the door. Problem solved!

Most difficult dementia behaviors are provoked. Part of being a good care partner is understanding this and learning to eliminate the events and stimulants that trigger problematic behavior. This is especially true during the late afternoon and evening. Keep a journal, learn the behaviors, times, and patterns, and take pre-emptive action.

And don't forget that *We all deserve the best!*

Chapter Twenty-Three:
Is Alzheimer's Hereditary?

Many of the people in my care partner support groups are men or women in their 50s or 60s who are caring for a parent with dementia. I often hear the questions, "Is Alzheimer's hereditary?" I can hear the concern in their voices, and what I know they are really asking me is, "Am I going to get it?" Their concern is understandable. The last thing they want is to end up where their parents are with this devastating disease.

Before we tackle the question of whether Alzheimer's is hereditary, lets return to the basics . . . to the definition of dementia.

First, dementia is *not* a disease. Dementia is the term we use to describe the various symptoms that result from Alzheimer's and other specific causes of dementia. These symptoms include memory loss, loss of peripheral vision, and reduced ability to hear and understand, which can result from both lost auditory function as well as loss of the ability to cognitively process a series of words. Other symptoms include loss of manual dexterity, loss of the ability to speak, and loss of basic sensory abilities, such as the ability to recognize heat or cold, hunger or thirst. Mood and personality changes can also be symptoms of dementia.

There are many specific diseases and health problems that can cause dementia, including brain injury. Some authorities say they have identified more than a hundred causes of dementia. So where does Alzheimer's fit in and why do we focus on it so much when discussing dementia?

Alzheimer's is a specific disease that is the cause of more than half of all dementia; some claim as much as 70 percent. This is why we talk so much about Alzheimer's. It has been called the disease of our time for good reason. With the Baby Boomer generation now entering the 70-plus age range, we are seeing a distinct increase in Alzheimer's. Unfortunately, this trend will continue for the next several decades.

Before tackling the topic of Alzheimer's and genetics, let's look briefly at the bigger picture with the question, "Is dementia hereditary?" Definitely, yes, in some cases it is. For example, Huntington's Disease leads to symptoms of dementia, and it definitely is hereditary. There are other specific diseases leading to dementia that are hereditary, but itemizing them is not the purpose of this column, nor would it be useful for people concerned about whether they are likely to get Alzheimer's.

The broad answer to the question about Alzheimer's and heredity is, "yes," there is a relationship. While scientists still have not definitively isolated what causes Alzheimer's, it is known that there is a genetic factor connected with a specific gene that seems to contribute to onset of the disease. If both you and a parent with Alzheimer's have this gene, it slightly increases the likelihood that you will contract the disease. If both of your parents have this gene, your likelihood of contracting Alzheimer's is higher.

But, by way of some reassurance, two facts are very important: 1) the increase in your likelihood to "inherit" Alzheimer's is miniscule, and 2) this gene showing up in two first-degree relatives does *not* guarantee that you will get the disease. It is what scientists call a "risk gene," not a "deterministic gene." You can take some reassurance in the fact that "familial Alzheimer's" represents less than three percent of the population living with Alzheimer's.

To put things in perspective, let's remember that everyone is already at risk of developing Alzheimer's; no one is immune! You can contract this disease whether or not anyone else in your family has it, but people who have a parent, a brother, or a sister with Alzheimer's have a slightly higher risk, especially if their Alzheimer's is the type called "early onset."

I have said before that I think early screening is important. If you are not showing symptoms, but still are worried because Alzheimer's is in your family, it is doubly important to get screened. At least, you will be establishing a base line for brain performance, which can be monitored as you age. There are research companies that provide thorough and free screening.

In summary, while heredity may play a role in contracting Alzheimer's, it is relatively insignificant. Whether you are concerned about the loved one you are caring for, or about your own future, please remember my motto: *"We all deserve the best."*

Chapter Twenty-Four:
Drumming and dementia

Ritual drumming is deeply rooted in the Japanese culture, which has been presented to the West in worldwide tours by the famous Kodo Drummers. Now, researchers in Japan are studying the effects of drumming on dementia, which they believe can impede cognitive decline.

Dr. Miyazaki Atsuko has conducted a controlled experiment in which patients with moderate to advanced dementia joined groups that participated in supervised drumming for 30 minutes, three times a week, for three months. Afterward, members of this group scored more than two points higher on a standard cognitive test when compared to a control group that did not participate in drumming.

In addition to cognitive improvement, the participants showed improved physical dexterity, and many experienced weight loss. Clearly, drumming reduced their symptoms of dementia. To see a video about Dr. Miyazaki's experiment, go to https://www.youtube.com/watch?v=FX87ay94 NFE.

This does not surprise me. We have known for years that music can have beneficial effects on individuals living with dementia, and rhythm is the foundation of music. To see an impressive demonstration of this fact, I urge you to watch the movie "Alive Inside," a documentary that features a man with advanced dementia named Henry.

Henry is unresponsive, very nearly comatose, and cannot answer a simple question or create a simple sentence. Headphones playing his favorite kind of music are placed on his head, and the response is immediate. Henry raises his head, opens his eyes, begins to move rhythmically, and begins to sing.

After a few minutes of listening to music, Henry is articulate and can carry on a conversation. He talks about his love of music and performs a hilariously accurate impersonation of one of his favorites, Cab Calloway. Henry reminisces about attending dances as a young man, and explains, "Music is love." To see a video about Henry's remarkable transformation, go to https://www.youtube.com/watch?v=8HLEr-zP3fc.

Unfortunately, the change will not last and Henry will lapse back into his state of silence, isolation, and inaction. But for a period of time, the effects of music are simply stunning. The research I reviewed about the drumming experiment in Japan did not present any data that would suggest that there was a residual or long-term benefit, and I suspect there is not.

We must remind ourselves that dementia is caused by a physical and progressive degradation of the brain. Brain tissue is dying, and no therapy has yet been found to actually impede this process or restore brain function in the long term.

But this does not mean that music and rhythm therapies are useless. To the contrary, they are quite effective, inexpensive, and they have none of the side effects, cost, or hazards of pharmacological therapies. We must remind ourselves that at this stage of our scientific knowledge, and in the absence of a "cure," the greatest gift we can give our loved ones with dementia is an improved quality of life, even if it is only temporary. Music and even pure rhythm without tonal qualities provide this.

Let us use and celebrate these simple therapies and remember that we all deserve the best.

Chapter Twenty-Five:
Don't become a 'secondary patient'

According to the National Institute of Health, for individuals over 65 years of age who are in family care, the average age of their care partner is 63!

When we start families, we are usually in our late teens or early 20s, and we bring a child into the world whom we know will require around-the-clock attention for more than a year. But we are young, we are strong, and we have energy.

This is not the case with family care partners for loved ones with Alzheimer's and other forms of dementia. Our sixties and seventies are not a good time in our lives to take on a new task that will require our attention 24/7.

What's worse, the person to whom we give care is not a small child that we can carry in the crook of one arm. It is an adult who in many cases is heavy and strong. And, unlike the relatively brief total dependency of an infant, we can expect that our task of care can last eight to twelve years! And add to this the fact that a child's skills and cognition will improve. With your loved one with dementia, it is just the opposite. The task of care only becomes more challenging as time goes by.

Little wonder then, that many care partners end up unwell to the extent that some may die before the person they are caring for. This is the worst possible outcome for a family living with dementia. And if they don't succumb, care partners may end up a 'secondary patient' whose physical and emotional condition leaves them less capable of performing their duties.

There are many things a care partner can do to protect their own physical and emotional wellbeing.

The first is that you must seek help. Some care partners believe that they are solely obligated to take care of their loved one. This is a dangerous attitude that can only lead to isolation and exhaustion. Seek the support of a friend or relative to spell you with simple tasks, even if they do not involve the direct care of your loved one.

When someone asks if they can do something to help you, give them a task, no matter how small or insignificant it may seem. If you do this, you will become more comfortable with asking for help in the future, and this is good.

One of the best ways to take care of yourself is to attend care partner support groups. Those who are on a similar journey may have useful advice for how you can keep a focus on *your* health. And, they can serve as friendly monitors to tell you when they hear the words or see the signs that indicate that you are neglecting yourself and succumbing to physical and mental exhaustion. They can become your sense of perspective.

As a care partner, you must have time to yourself. There are both free and paid services that provide respite or day care for your loved one.

Educate yourself about the disease and your role as a care partner. There are many books on the topic, and in Citrus County especially there are lots of free workshops for family care partners. Some of these focus on ways you can make your task easier and less stressful. We can also recommend the "Savvy Caregiver" workshop provided by Florida Elder Options.

Get your legal paperwork in order. Changes in your loved one's medical condition can happen fast, and a time of crisis is no time to begin to worry about whether wills, advanced directives, and other legal matters are in order. There is a free workshop called "Five

Wishes" that can show you how simple and inexpensive this process can be.

If your loved one was in the armed forces, it is possible there are veteran's benefits that can help you financially or provide respite and support. Contact the local Veteran's Administration office to see what is available.

Put in layers of protection to keep your loved one safe. This can include proper locks and alarms, and a scent kit that can help searchers find your loved one if he or she wanders and becomes lost. The scent kit is available from Find-M-Friends (www.findmfriends.com) or Coping with Dementia (www.coping.today). And don't forget to register your loved one with the Citrus County Sheriff's Office (http://www.sheriffcitrus.org/register-someone-with-autism-dementia.php).

These measures may not give you respite today, but they are pre-emptive measures that will reduce the likelihood of a future crisis. Peace of mind is a big part of caring for yourself.

Alzheimer's care is not a sprint that will be over quickly. It is more like a marathon, so you have to pace yourself and maintain a quality of life for both you and your loved one over a long period of time.

So, please pay as much attention to your medical needs as to those of the person you are caring for. Keep your medical appointments and check-ups. The best care you can provide for your loved one is to care for yourself. And remember that *you both deserve the best.*

Chapter Twenty-Six:
Art and music provide
beneficial therapy

We've all seen pictures of the human brain. It is symmetrical and divided down the middle. One half looks pretty much like a mirror image of the other half, but they actually have very different functions.

The left side is "wired" to contain and manage language, mathematics, and other functions we might describe as "rational" thinking. The right side houses music, rhythm, and other functions we might describe as "creative." You've probably heard people say that engineers and scientists are "left-brained" people, and artists and musicians are "right-brained" people. This is a vast oversimplification, but it is useful information to know when caring for someone living with Alzheimer's or some other form of dementia.

Another useful fact to understand is that Alzheimer's attacks the left hemisphere of the brain first. The ability to speak, understand complex sentences, and solve problems are often some of the abilities lost early on, along with short-term memory.

When a person with dementia is not able to describe what they need, we often conclude that they can no longer communicate. This is a wrong assumption because there are ways to communicate other than language. Let me give you an example that was a powerful learning moment for me.

I was managing a memory care facility, and we were working with some of our residents who were painting pictures. We were outdoors, and as the sun went down, one woman painted a simple horizon across her paper with half of a bright orange disc on the horizon. As we looked at and complimented her on her art, she wrapped her arms around her body and moved like she was shivering. She was not just painting the sun; she was telling us she was cold because the sun was setting!

This was some pretty sophisticated and successful communication even though she did not have language at her command. Often, there is a lot more going on in that head than we realize, and it is *we,* the care partners, who are failing to communicate if we try to hold our people with dementia to "normal" communication methods and standards.

Something else we know is that Alzheimer's attacks the right side of the brain later than the left. This means that creative functions are intact and still active after rational functions have become seriously degraded. Music and rhythm are still there, and I have seen evidence of this when a man who could no longer construct a sentence was able to flawlessly sing two verses of a hymn!

Music can be very therapeutic. It can sooth an agitated person, spark memories, stimulate brain activity – even in later stages of the dementia – and bring joy, which is clearly evident in facial expressions and body movement.

The kind of music is important. The best may be golden oldies, toe-tapping beats, easy listening, and religious hymns. As we grow up, the music we remember most is what we listened to between the ages of eight and 20. This can be useful in selecting music from their past, but your loved one will tell you what he or she likes. Just watch when you play different types of music, then zero in on the songs and styles that create the most positive response.

The same is true of art. Painting, drawing, and other media can help people with dementia express themselves, just as I described above with the woman who painted the setting sun.

In practicing art therapy, keep instructions to a minimum. This is about creativity, not painting a masterpiece. Do it together. Hold hands and demonstrate brush strokes, then let your loved one take over. If you don't like the colors they have chosen or what they are doing, keep it to yourself. This process is to please and stimulate them, not you. Talk to them in a positive way about what they are doing; praise their work.

Like music, art can be calming, stimulate brain activity, help maintain manual dexterity, and bring joy and satisfaction. I can't help but believe that the woman who painted the setting sun was very grateful when we – the persons allegedly with the big brains – finally caught on to what she was telling us, and took her indoors where it was warm.

Art and music therapy work because people with dementia do not lose their feelings. This is a fact that can be proven through brain scans. Even in late stages of dementia when most of the brain has "gone cold" with lack of chemical or electrical activity, we can see that the organs that manage the emotions (the amygdala) remain active. If you need convincing, just watch the movie "Alive Inside." Even in final stages when a person is essentially comatose, you can see remarkable response to music and rhythm!

As I often remind you, *We all deserve the best!* Art and music therapy are proven ways to make things better for both the care partner and their loved one living with dementia.

Chapter Twenty-Seven:
Finding resources: Let your fingers do the walking

Caring for a person living with Alzheimer's and other forms of dementia can be a stressful and exhausting task, and hands-on care for your loved one is only a portion of that task. It also involves finding information, resources, services, and support that can help you become a better and less stressed care partner.

When I was caring for my husband Albert, I found the search for help frustrating and difficult; sometimes infuriating. I even wrote a long letter describing my needs and problems to my State Senator's office. I got back a campaign bumper sticker!

Nearly a decade later, the task of locating resources remains difficult, but the internet has made it easier. What I want to do in this column is provide resources where your "fingers can do the walking." This is the slogan we used to use for the Yellow Pages (remember those?), but now I am referring to your fingers going to your keyboard. I hope to point out some very helpful web sites, beginning with national and moving to local resources.

Let me first suggest that you go to the web site for the National Institute of Health (www.nih.gov). This web site provides a wealth of information. At the top of the page is a button entitled "Health Information" which will lead you to a drop-down menu that includes a search feature. Write in the box "Alzheimer's and dementia" and you will be directed to a long list of useful articles on the subject.

In conducting this kind of search, you will need to try to focus on the kind of information useful to you, because you can get lost in medical minutia that goes far beyond your need to know as a care partner. I tell care partners that you need to have a basic understanding of what is happening to your person with dementia, but you should never forget that your job is to care for the person, not become a medical expert on the disease.

In the NIH drop down menu you will also see a button that says "Health Services Finder." This will take you to a separate web site called Healthfinder.gov. There is also a button that says "Clear Health from NIH" which will take you to a page with links to information about caring for a person with Alzheimer's. You can also order many free publications through the NIH web site.

There is also a lot of helpful information on the National Caregiving Foundation's web site (www.caregiving.org). For Alzheimer's and dementia, it offers a free support kit. It is a very substantial ring binder that can help you become informed and stay organized. It is free!

The Alzheimer's Association web site (www.alz.org) is an excellent source of information with lots of useful statistics and articles. I find that this site is very good at covering tough and complex topics in a way that we laymen can understand.

For example, one of most common questions I get is "Is Alzheimer's hereditary?" The simple answer is "yes," but this answer is overly simple and can lead to unnecessary fear or concern. The full answer is far more complicated, and this site explains it better than I have seen anywhere else.

I can't say enough about Teepasnow.com. Teepa Snow is a leading dementia theorist and practitioner whom I have studied under, and in my opinion, she teaches the highest and most effective standards of care available today. What is great about Teepa's site is her videos that explain and demonstrate her techniques of compassionate care. You can also find these on YouTube and Tik Tok.

Individuals living with dementia lose manual dexterity, peripheral vision, and other sensory abilities, in addition to judgment and memory. They can be easier to care for, and their quality of life can become better through the use of special clothing and products that are available on the internet. Try the Alzheimer's Store (www.alzstore.com) or Buck and Buck/Alzheimer's (https://www.buckandbuck.com/shop-by-need/alzheimers-clothing.html).

Now let's move to the State level where I will recommend the web site for Elder Options (http://agingresources.org), a clearing house for a great wealth of information and services provided by the State of Florida. Elder Options not only offers information on-line, but it conducts free workshops all over the State, including its popular Savvy Caregiver Training. Some people learn better one-on-one than searching through web sites, so these workshops bring the information to the care partner, including those of us in Citrus County.

A schedule of educational events can be found on the site.

This is also the agency in Florida that works to prevent elder abuse, neglect, and exploitation. Anyone who has concerns in this area, either in the home or under professional care, can call 800-962-2873.

If you are already in the search for an appropriate Assisted Living Facility or Home Health Care provider, you can find helpful guidance on the Florida Agency for Health Care Administration web site (www.ahca.myflorida.com). This is a licensing and regulatory agency, and from its web site you can draw conclusions about the quality of care at facilities or home care providers that you are considering. On AHCA's menu bar you will find "Find a Facility," and clicking it will take you to "Consumer Guides" and "Compare Healthcare Facilities." There are also portals where you can report complaints and fraud.

Moving to the local level, Citrus County Senior Services is a great resource. Go to the Citrus County Board of County Commissioners web site (www.citrusbocc.com) and on the right side of the front page you will see a box that says "Quick Links." A click here will give you a drop-down menu that takes you to "Senior

Care Services." Quick links will also take you to "Veteran Services," which can be useful for care partners whose loved ones have served in the military.

Care partners will face important legal considerations, such as healthcare surrogacy, obtaining a Durable Power of Attorney, and determining whether to create a DNR (do not resuscitate) order. These decisions may involve working with an elder care attorney, and often we procrastinate too long over these issues. Ideally, they should be addressed while your loved one is still cognitive. A good starting place that will cost you nothing is Hospice of Citrus County and the Nature Coast (https://hospiceofcitrus.org/). This non-profit organization offers a free workshop called "Five Wishes" that is a great starting place to get your loved one's affairs and your own affairs in order.

Let me add here that many people simply do not understand the role of hospice and the services available. The common belief is that hospice involves only end-of-life services, but many hospices offer much more, including home care. Contact them; they will tell you about these services and what it will take for your loved one to qualify.

Moving now to the local level, let's not forget what a great resource we have right here in Citrus County with Find-M' Friends which, in cooperation with the Key Training Center, manufacture Out of Harm's Way Scent Kits that can save lives when people with dementia wander and become lost. You can call 352-613-3486, 352-422-3663, or the Sheriff's Office. They are free, but a donated is requested.

Speaking of the Citrus County Sheriff's Office, it offers a Special Needs Person Registration System, a resource not yet found in many other jurisdictions. Just go to their web site (www.sheriffcitrus.org) and click the button "How do I?" This will create a drop-down menu where you can click "Autism/Dementia" to register on line.

Finally, you can find local resources at the Coping with Dementia web site (www.coping.today). In the interest of full disclosure, I must advise you that this is the web site for my company. It has a listing for upcoming free workshops and care partner support groups. It also archives my columns that have appeared in the Citrus County Chronicle.

In the upper left-hand corner of the front page of this site you will find a button that says "See Who's Dementia Friendly." This will lead you to a great and special resource that most counties in America do not have. It is a listing of the many businesses and churches that have undergone training to be certified to provide Dementia Friendly service.

Finally, I also distribute a monthly e-newsletter that contains up-to-date information of support groups, workshops, special events, and services. To receive this newsletter, just e-mail me at deb@coping.today, and I will place you on the list. This list is confidential and never sold or shared with anyone else, and you can un-subscribe any time you like.

Don't forget that even during the sometimes-difficult task of finding help and resources, "We all deserve the best!"

Editor's Note: While parts of this column focus on resources available in Florida, readers should be aware that other states have equivalent services and agencies.

Chapter Twenty-Eight:
Hug Therapy; It really works!

When my husband Albert contracted Alzheimer's Disease, he was otherwise healthy and very physically fit. The disease took away his ability to speak very early, which meant he was mobile but unable to express himself through language.

People with Alzheimer's are still going to try to express their desires and needs, and if they can't do it with language, they will find other ways. Unfortunately, we often see this as "acting out," and conclude they are combative or dangerous. This is how Albert was branded. Although for me he remained a gentle and loving man, the people in professional care facilities advised me that he was "combative."

He was kicked out of three memory care facilities, not just within days or weeks, but sometimes within hours! I would no sooner place him and return home when I would get the phone call, "If you don't come and get him now, we are going to Baker Act him!"

Eventually, I found a small memory care facility run by a wonderful couple named Joan and Tony who practiced a totally different approach to dementia care that I would later learn to call "Person-centered Compassionate Care." At the time, they told me, "We promise he will never be turned out. We will love him here through the rest of his life." At that moment, I had no idea what they were talking about. During my long search for a memory care facility that would keep Albert, I had not once heard any professional in dementia care use the word "love."

Here, Albert was treated with kindness and respect. When he walked into the room, Joan or Tony would hold out their arms and say, "Good morning, Mr. Albert." This went on for several days, then finally, one day Albert held out his arms, ready to accept a hug.

At this wonderful place, Albert never had a disruptive moment and he was taken off all of the psychotropic medications that others had used to try to control him. He lived quietly, smiled, and was always ready to accept a hug. His final months appeared to be the happiest and most peaceful days he had experienced in years.

At this moment, you may be asking, "Hugs? Are you kidding me? You think this disease can be managed with hugs?" Yes, to a certain extent it can. As an effective caregiving tool, hugs should be taken very seriously. They not only express compassion and respect for the person living with dementia, but they provide concrete emotional and physiological benefits that have been identified through many years of research.

Just Google "Hug Therapy" or "Hugs for Health" and see what you get. You will be surprised by the amount and depth of research that confirms the therapeutic power of hugging. There is even a series of books by Kathleen Keating about how and why hugs have positive results on IQ, aging, self-esteem, and emotional wellbeing.

Hugging can reduce stress, anxiety, depression, loneliness, and fear. It has been shown that babies who receive lots of hugging turn out to be less stressed as adults. Hugs benefit the immune system and increase the release of pleasure and comfort-giving hormones like Oxytocin, Dopamine, and Serotonin. Hugging has been shown to reduce infection and is beneficial for both the giver and the receiver.

Hugs also build relationships. When I was the administrator at a memory care community, I was a big believer and user of hug therapy. After I left this job to start my own company, I went back to visit three months later. Not only did people stand up and hold out their arms when I walked in, but some said, "Miss Debby, where have you been?" These were people with dementia who even remembered my name!

This experience reminded me of the words of the great American poet Maya Angelou. To paraphrase: "People will forget what you said, people will forget what you did, but people will never forget how you made them feel."

I have learned that while people are robbed of many of their senses and abilities by dementia, they do not lose their feelings. And this is another reason why hugs work. They work on a physiological level, but they also communicate on an emotional level that enables you to give your loved one more dignity, comfort, and joy than they will ever get from any drug.

Your loved one deserves hugs because *We all deserve the best!*

Chapter Twenty-Nine:
Alzheimer's not caused by aging

The other day, I read an article about health and longevity that contained the assertion, "The single biggest cause of Alzheimer's Disease is aging." This is absolutely wrong, and it represents a logical fallacy that we see all too often among so-called experts and suppliers of products and therapies that they claim will reverse, slow, or even cure dementia.

The nature of this logical fallacy is to confuse coincidence with cause and effect. Coincidence, by definition, is, "a striking occurrence of two or more events at one time apparently by mere chance." When we jump to the conclusion that one was the cause of the other, we have taken an illogical leap that can lead to misunderstandings and even harmful conclusions.

This kind of assertion bothers me a lot because it creates unnecessary fear in our aging population. Yes, Alzheimer's is "age related," but it is not caused by the aging process. It is a specific identifiable disease of the brain that some will get, but many will not, no matter how old they become. The great majority of people live out their lives without contracting Alzheimer's Disease.

In fact, according to the Alzheimer's Association, one in ten Americans over the age of 65 has Alzheimer's. This means that 90 percent of people over the age of 65 do not have Alzheimer's, which is a commanding majority.

It is true that the percentage of those with Alzheimer's goes higher as we age beyond 65, but this does not mean that advancing age is causing it. It is simply evidence that what is causing dementia has had more time to develop. "Age equals Alzheimer's" is an erroneous conclusion!

It would be convenient if we could make these simple one-on-one linkages, because then it would mean we are dealing with a simpler problem. But, at this juncture in our medical development, Alzheimer's Disease and other causes of dementia are anything but simple. At present, research is leading us toward more questions and greater complexity; not yet toward solutions.

Alzheimer's, we have believed for some time, is caused by "plaques" and "tangles" in the brain that interfere with neuro-connections that are basic to the brain's function. However, we have learned that these features alone may not cause cognitive decline or the other symptoms associated with dementia.

First, many of us have the plaques and tangles years before any sign of dementia begins to emerge, and we have also found that there are people in the Alzheimer's "age range;" 65 and older, who have the plaques and tangles but no symptoms of the disease.

So, what sets it off? What triggers the disease that results in the atrophy and devastation of the brain and its functions? We don't yet know. While the plaques and tangles may be a precursor or by-product, they alone do not appear to be the cause.

I feel that too often our beliefs about Alzheimer's are based on fear and opinion rather than logic and facts, and this can be very counterproductive to focusing on what we can do in the here-and-now to make life better for people, and their care partners, living with dementia.

Teepa Snow, the dementia practitioner I study under, says, "Until there is a cure, there's care!" At the current state of research, this statement should be our mantra; the focal point that directs our energy to helping others and achieving the things we can achieve.

I prefer to leave the discussion of cause and cure to the scientists and medical experts who are qualified for the task. I simply am not qualified in this field, but what I can do in the meantime is try to provide the resources, teach the techniques of effective care, and promote the philosophy of person-centered compassionate care that can help people today; not is some possibly distant future when we actually have a cure.

We all hope to see that day, but until then we have a lot of work to do to keep our loved ones with dementia safe, social, and with the dignity that provides them the best quality of life we possibly can. And the last thing we should do is tell people living in their senior years that aging is going to give them Alzheimer's! They, like us, *All deserve the best.*

Chapter 30:
Help for Care Partner burnout

Many times, I have heard care partners in my support groups say, "Sometimes I wonder which one of us has the dementia!" This has led us to use the term – sometimes jokingly or ironically – "Stress Induced Dementia," although there is really no such thing in the literal sense. But the term well expresses a level of care partner exhaustion when we begin to forget, lose things, and make bad decisions, as if we too have dementia.

Of course, so called "Stress Induced Dementia" is not really dementia because it does not come from permanent, physical brain change. We can also call it "burnout," and, fortunately, we can restore ourselves through seeking help, rest, better diet, meditation, and other practices of healthy self-care. Unlike real dementia, it can be reversed and eventually "cured."

Learning to recognize the warning signs of caregiver burnout is the first step toward seeking a solution. Here are some feelings and behaviors to watch for.

*Isolating yourself from friends and your loved ones, or from activities you previously enjoyed.

*Losing patience, becoming intolerant, and taking out your frustration on your loved one or others.
*Experiencing uncharacteristic outbursts of anger.
*Feelings of depression, anxiety, hopelessness, moodiness, irritability, and sleeplessness.
*The inability to make decisions; feeling scattered and unable to concentrate.
*Changes in appearance, losing weight, neglecting hygiene.
*Inability to undertake routine daily tasks, such as financial management or home cleaning and maintenance.

Many of your routine activities of daily living were shared with your loved one now living with dementia.   Now, your partner is no longer able to help. It is natural that you are overwhelmed.

Indeed, you may have a huge problem, but let me suggest that it can be approached like any large problem. Try to break it down into smaller tasks that are individually more manageable. This is a process where a care partner support group can give you a lot of help. Some of them have already gone through the process and come out the other side whole and successful. They know what you are going through.

Look for the little tasks that you may think have nothing to do with your actual care partnering responsibilities. Taking out the garbage, tending the lawn and gardens, walking the dog, washing the car, shopping; and seek help from friends, relatives, or neighbors to carry out these duties. This is the process of breaking your overwhelming problem into smaller manageable problems.

Journaling can be priceless in breaking down your problem. Make a list of duties you have begun to neglect or don't have time for. Many of us resist journaling because we think we don't have the time. The time you put into journaling will be retrieved many times over when you have a list of small, manageable tasks for which you can seek help.

It is easier to ask for help when you are asking for small things, and it is easier to accept help when someone offers to do small things. Through this process, you can build a "team" of three or four people who, collectively, begin to remove a bigger burden – piece by piece -- from your shoulders.

During a time of care partner burnout, it is important to bring some joy and humor back into your life. Again, this is the role of a care partner support group. Their perspective is different from yours, but they have been where you are now, and some have learned to recognize and laugh at the absurdities that dementia can bring into our lives. Having a trusted care partner make you laugh is the most restorative medicine you will ever know.

When you recognize you are in a state of burnout, or when you see it coming, realize that the most important thing you can do for yourself is to NOT be alone. There are so many others who have traveled this path. They understand, they know the pain, and they are usually ready to help.

Please do not look at seeking help as a weakness. To the contrary, it takes tremendous strength and trust in your fellow travelers. And remember that dementia care is not a sprint; it is a marathon. This long journey becomes easier when you think of it as a relay race where you can from time-to-time hand off the baton to a fellow runner. Seek and accept help with the belief that we in this journey *all deserve the best.*

Chapter 31:
Until there's a cure . . .

My primary training is in The Positive Approach to Care®, developed by Teepa Snow and sometimes called the *Snow Method* or *Snow Approach*. Teepa's slogan is, "Until there's a cure, there's care." This trips nicely off the tongue and seems too obvious to be profound, but there is so much more meaning in this statement than we might see at first glance.

I had this brought home to me recently when I had the opportunity to attend a two-day conference in Orlando organized by the Alzheimer's Association, the Florida Department of Health, and others. This event brought together some of the top people in the field, including scientists who are conducting research for a cure.

I was overwhelmed with the amount of knowledge imparted, but came away feeling quite unsatisfied, for two reasons. First, we heard nothing very optimistic about the state of research for a cure. The more research we conduct, the more questions – not answers – we seem to uncover. Fundamental theories about the cause of the disease that have directed research for two decades are now being abandoned as dead ends! I did not see even a glimmer of that hoped-for cure at the end of the tunnel.

The second reason was that I heard so little about care. The Alzheimer's Association and the Florida Department of Elder Affairs offered some really good workshops about care techniques and resources available to care partners. But there seems to be so little attention, or money, directed toward the development of an art or science of better care. By this I mean, how do we better deploy to caregivers what we already know, and what shall we do to research and develop new techniques of care to improve the quality of life for both the care partners and those living with dementia?

It is true that the U.S. Congress has recently approved historic increases for support of Alzheimer's cure and care programs, and this is wonderful evidence that our public education and awareness programs are working. But when I speak of better funding for "care," I am talking about money for innovative care research in addition to the increased funding for the training, education, and respite programs that are already available.

Don't misunderstand me. I am all for the research for a cure, and I hope one day soon it will succeed. One speaker at the conference expressed his enthusiasm for cure research by excitedly predicting, "There is a person living on Earth today who will be cured of Alzheimer's!" Indeed, we hope, but I thought sadly to myself, "If this assertion were even true, it could be another 90 years! Would it not be better to also more aggressively pursue better funding for higher standards of care in the here-and-now?"

In addition to a continuation of heavy spending toward a cure, here is how I would like to see us allocate more funding toward care:

I would like to see more research into the behavioral psychology of individuals living with dementia. Can we learn more about what motivates their behaviors and thereby learn ways to serve and communicate with them more effectively, compassionately, and less disruptively?

I would like to see money spent on evidence-based research into compassionate techniques of care such as hug therapy and humor therapy. We know they work. How can we better understand and develop them so more care partners – both family and professional – know how to apply them?

I would like to see research into kinder and gentler non-pharmacological methods of mood management. After all, none of the psychotropic drugs used on people with dementia were ever intended for dementia, and sometimes they bring more problems than solutions.

I would like to see publicly-funded dementia hotlines, manned by volunteers who have received extensive training in understanding the personality and behavioral changes that people with dementia experience. These skilled facilitators would be on hand to de-escalate difficult situations so that deputies do not have to be called to Baker Act people who have no control over their behaviors.

And speaking of the Baker Act; this is a whole topic unto itself. Significant resources should be allocated to updating and reforming this process so that people with dementia are not treated like drunks, criminals, and drug addicts, or thrown into chaotic and sometimes violent populations that only escalate their confusion and anxiety to a level worse than when they arrived.

I would like to see state legislatures and regulating agencies raise the minimum standards of care required for professional providers. These have not been updated in more than 15 years, which I believe is quite unacceptable.

I would like to see more funding for public and private-sector agencies to provide workshops for family care partners since many of us will never be able to afford professional care.

Finally, I would like to see well-planned and funded research and learning institutes devoted entirely to the topic of better care. Through these, we can produce a whole new generation of young, compassionate medical professionals who understand they are dealing with people, not just a disease.

By all means, let's keep chasing that cure. But let us not forget that until there is a cure, there is care. No, let me rephrase that: "Until there is a cure, there is ONLY care!"

Chapter 32:
Hospice not just about end of life

While conducting workshops and counseling families coping with dementia, I often see negative reactions when I mention the word "hospice." This is unfortunate, because hospice offers many services useful to families living with dementia.

Many believe that hospice provides end-of-life services only. To the contrary, hospice can provide a wide range of valuable services to individuals and families both before and after the death of a loved one.

Perhaps the worst misunderstanding I've heard is that hospice somehow accelerates the dying process. This is simply not true. For end-of-life clients, hospice provides physical, emotional, and spiritual support while nature takes its course.

In these situations, hospice provides interdisciplinary care teams that can include medical directors, chaplains, nurses, social workers, home health aides, bereavement specialists, and volunteers to provide a wide range of support. These teams don't "take over;" rather they work with your own physician to address your family's needs.

But the role of hospice does not end when your loved one dies. Beyond end-of-life support, hospice provides many additional services of real value to care partners and their loved ones. Many hospice organizations provide bereavement counseling for the whole family, including both adults and youngsters who have experienced the loss of a loved one.

Many provide services tailor-made to specific constituencies, such as veterans services, grief and recovery camps for youth, services to families who are dealing with loved ones with dementia, and even networks for widows and widowers to help them remain active in the community during their time of loss.

As Jonathan Beard, Community Education Manager at Hospice of Citrus and the Nature Coast, told me, "Hospice is not about dying; it is about living. It provides emotional, physical, and spiritual comfort for those in their final days, but it continues to be available to those who must live on; for the families and individuals who must move beyond the loss of a loved one."

But because many have an overly narrow understanding of the role of hospice, too few take advantage of their broader range of services. Beard states, "Typically, people wait too long to seek our services. Not only can we help them earlier in the family's journey toward the end of life, but we can stay with them afterward to help them move more successfully to a new normal."

As care partners, it is important that we understand the full range of services provided by the various hospice organizations. They are not just for the individual who is under care or approaching the end of life. They can be helpful to their families and care partners as well, and *We all deserve the best*.

Chapter 33:
Danger from the dementia perspective

Daily, we are surrounded by danger. There is that throw rug with the corner turned up; that low foot stool we might trip over; the sharp corner of the table or desk we could run into. How about those power tools, solvents, and insecticides in the garage? There are sharp knives in the kitchen, and under the kitchen sink are toxic cleaning agents.

Medicines in the bathroom can harm us if overdosed. And there's the firearm in the dresser drawer or the top shelf of the closet. Many of us have a swimming pool where we can easily drown ourselves. And let's not forget the car or motorcycle we frequently use for travel! It is a lot of weight and horsepower just waiting to maim or kill us or someone else if not properly managed.

It seems to be a scary world we live in. But not really. Over a long period of time, we have learned from parenting, school, reading instructions, safety classes, specialized education, and even occasionally from the School of Hard Knocks to integrate all of these dangerous things into a safe and manageable life. In fact, we have acquired this dangerous stuff because it makes our life easier when we know how to use it safely and sanely.

But when we become a care partner for a friend or loved one living with dementia, we must understand that all of this learning will gradually (or sometimes rapidly) disappear, and their world will become a potentially deadly place indeed! As good care partners, we must relearn to look at the world from the perspective of what it would be to us without all that parenting, training, and education. We must re-envision it through *their* eyes, and this isn't always easy to do.

When I was caring for my husband Albert, believing that he was still able to function alone at home while I was at work, I one day noticed that the ceramic bottom and sides of his favorite coffee cup had become rough and appeared to be wearing away. After a little exploration beneath the kitchen sink, I discovered to my horror that he had been scrubbing out the coffee stains with an industrial de-greasing agent. Where he got it, I'm not sure; and how he had not already poisoned himself, I do not know!

This brings us to our first lesson about danger from the dementia perspective. People who are losing their ability to think logically or use good judgment will continue to be curious; often very curious! Don't think for a minute that you can hide anything from them that is not locked away, or that they will simply ignore those dangerous chemicals, pesticides, and solvents on the shelf in the garage.

The world of dementia becomes dangerous for two very different reasons. The first is that they are forgetting everything they learned about how to take care of themselves and handle potentially dangerous agents and objects.

You have to accept this fact and anticipate it. You cannot wait until they make a mistake before you make changes to improve or assure their safety. In my care partner support groups, I often ask the following question: "Do you put up a fence around your backyard pool after your toddler shows you he can fall in?" Of course not!

But there is another reason that the world becomes dangerous for a person living with dementia. Everyone knows that dementia destroys our memory, but many do not realize it degrades all of our senses and, over time, our physical abilities.

For example, with dementia we lose our peripheral vision and eventually our depth perception. Our ability to hear and comprehend also changes. We lose the ability to process the words in a sentence and we develop "white noise" and even phantom sounds that confuse us and interfere with our ability to take in auditory information accurately and usefully.

Combined, our peripheral vision and our hearing provide a lot of our safety. With normal vision, you do not unwittingly turn into a car overtaking in the next lane because you can *see* it even when it is not yet beside you. And while you may not think much about it at the moment, you can probably also *hear* it approaching.

The loss of these abilities will cause a person with dementia to put themselves in harm's way, to not see that loose throw rug or that stool they can trip over, or the sharp corner of that desk or table.

Dementia also degrades our olfactory function. We lose our sense of smell, which can lead to eating outdated and bad food, especially among those living alone. Or it might cause a person living with dementia to not realize that something is burning.

Dementia also takes away our manual dexterity, which means a person may no longer be able to safely handle tools that they once routinely used. In addition, dementia can degrade our balance and coordination skills.

For the care partner who wants to keep their friend or loved one safe, there is really a lot to learn. Let me suggest two courses of action. I offer free workshops called the ABC of Dementia where we discuss the factors of judgment, cognition, vision, hearing, and other forms of sensory function in greater detail. Contact me to learn when and where the next workshop will take place.

In addition, let me suggest the Senior Resources/Aging in Place web site that provides guidelines for home assessment for safety. Go to www.seniorresource.com/ageinpl.htm#assess.

And finally, especially in matters of keeping your friend or loved one safe, let's remember that we all deserve to be safe, and *We all deserve the best.*

Chapter 34:
The Big Three misconceptions about dementia

Dementia is a widely misunderstood condition. Although there are many misconceptions that lead to mistakes in care-giving, there are three serious and common misconceptions that I confront time and again in counseling and conducting training for care partners.

The first, and most common, and possibly the misconception that leads to more trouble than any other, is the belief that people with dementia are combative and unpredictable by nature of the disease, and therefor dangerous. This belief leads to isolation and loneliness for the person living with dementia because others are afraid of them.

Although people living with dementia receive information through their five senses differently from healthy people, and while it takes a person with dementia longer to process this information, I believe they are like the rest of us in that they react to their environment and what is happening to them at any given moment. Their behavior is not random, and the great majority of them do not strike out for no reason.

It takes education and training to understand how persons with dementia perceive the world around them, but once a care partner has mastered a few key understandings, they realize people living with dementia behave the way they do for a reason. If they strike out, it is probably not without cause. Usually, it has been provoked by someone or something in their environment.

Knowing this enables us to adjust our behaviors to avoid unpleasant or combative incidents. And it is incumbent upon us as care partners to make the necessary adjustments. We have the ability to learn and change; the person with dementia does not.

Another of the Big Three misconceptions is that a person with dementia is delusional because they don't perceive the world the same way we do. This is a very unhelpful belief that will never lead to better care-giving or a productive relationship between the care partner and a person with dementia.

I did a column recently about how sometimes their past becomes their present. In their minds, they often seem to move to a previous period in their life. We can never understand completely what is going on in their minds, but a complete understand is not necessary. What is important is to accept the fact that their reality is as valid for them as ours is for us.

Once we adopt this attitude, we can learn to work with them within their reality by never arguing, refuting, dismissing, or trying to force them to see things the way we do. Attempting to make them see things our way never works, and can only end in strife and grief.

Again, as with all cases of responding to dementia behavior, we must accept that it is our responsibility as care partners to adjust and accommodate, because they cannot. Keep reminding yourself: "He's not trying to *give you* a hard time. He's *having* a hard time."

We know that dementia involves much more than memory loss. It also results in loss of language skills, loss of cognitive ability and executive function, and degradation of all five senses, including manual and small motor dexterity.

When we witness these changes, it is easy to conclude that a person living with dementia loses everything. This is the third great misconception. They do not lose everything because they do not lose their feelings. They do not lose their ability to experience joy and pain.

We know this not just from observation, but also through brain science. Brain scans reveal that when almost all of the brain of a person in advanced dementia has gone dark, the two small organs that manage our "feelings," the amygdala, are still functioning.

This is important for a care partner to understand, because it enables us to have a beneficial relationship with our loved one even up to the moment they close their eyes for the final time. In fact, in late-stage dementia, their ability to experience emotion is the *only* tool we have left to work with and through which to communicate.

Through their ability to experience emotions, we can work with music and gentle touch to reach them with messages of love, joy, and compassion. Their reaction may be only a small change of expression or a fluttering of an eyelid, but don't doubt that you are reaching them in a beneficial way.

Because they still have their feelings, music therapy becomes one of the most useful ways to create joy, peace, and comfort in a person in end-stage dementia.

To summarize, people living with dementia are not unpredictable and random in their behavior, their reality is as valid for them as ours is for us, and they retain their feelings even when other senses and abilities are gone. Working with these key understandings will enable us to be better and more compassionate care partners, resulting in less stress and anxiety for both parties.

And remember that *We all deserve the best.*

`Chapter 35:
Your relationship with
a care community

Although most Americans choose to care for their loved ones at home, many do not or cannot, but choose to entrust the task to an Assisted Living Facility (ALF), a Memory Care Community, or a Skilled Nursing Environment. While these differ in cost and services, for the sake of our discussion we will use the term ALF collectively.

There is a lot at stake when you choose placement for a loved one. The cost is significant, and you have essentially placed your loved one in the hands of strangers. The purpose of this column is to highlight some ways to build a relationship of respect and mutual trust with the ALF you have chosen.

*Read the contract and take it seriously – You will be presented a contract that may be as long as 60 pages. Read it and ask questions about anything you do not understand. Take it to an attorney if you feel you do not understand it. This will lay the foundation for a relationship of mutual respect since ALF management will see that you do not take your decision lightly.
*Your initial dialogue when you are making a decision about placement will be with a

Marketing representative. This is the time
you should ask any questions you have
about the contract, and it is also the time
when you should make your expectations
known about what your person needs and
how you expect him/her to be cared for.
This will lay the ground work for your
relationship with the ALF's top
management.

*Once you have selected your loved one's
new home, establish a relationship with is
top management. Insist on meeting the
Executive Director, and let him/her know
that you intend to build a productive and
team-based relationship.

*Don't be demanding or pushy. Be friendly,
polite, and business-like. Again, you are
laying the groundwork for a successful
experience for your loved one.

*Prior to your initial meeting with the E.D.,
be sure you understand the Patient's Bill of
Rights and Responsibilities. It should be in
your contract, and law requires the ALF to
post it in public view.

*Create a history of your loved one. This
can be a ring-binder containing information
about their career, their family, their
religion, their favorite things, etc. It should
include photographs and relevant news
clippings. Present this binder to the E.D. on
the occasion of your first meeting and let
him/her know that the individuals in charge

of your loved one's care are expected to know what it contains. Again, be friendly, humble, and businesslike. Don't be demanding or pushy. Your goal is to build mutual respect within your team.

*Ask the E.D. how often the ALF routinely reviews and updates a patient's Care Plan, or what kind of events or problems might trigger a review of the Care Plan. Emphasize again that you want your loved one to be considered a unique person with a unique history and unique needs, not just "Mr. Room 305." Let it be known – again, in a businesslike manner – that you expect to be involved in meetings where the Care Plan is reviewed and updated. Keep emphasizing that your loved one's care will be a partnership between you and the ALF's management.

*Do not interfere with the subordinate care staff. During your visits, be friendly, polite, and reinforce or praise their efforts when appropriate. But if you see something that concerns you, do not confront the care staff involved. Take your concerns to the E.D. who may encourage you to dialogue with the Director of Nursing. But do not involve yourself in the chain-of-command below the management level.

What if your best efforts do not get positive results? You have the option to file a complaint with the Florida Agency for Health Care Administration, or you can ask to describe your concerns to an ombudsman who serves under the Florida Department of Elder Affairs.

But, let us emphasize again that Job One is to build a productive and mutually respectful relationship with your chosen ALF. If you resort to AHCA or Elder Affairs, that relationship is probably already broken, or at least it will be! This is the course of last resort and should never be considered until you stand convinced that your best negotiating and interpersonal skills have failed.

As you work to establish a productive relationship with your chosen ALF, keep my favorite slogan in mind: "We all deserve the best!"

Chapter 36:
Resolving to become
a less-stressed care partner

As January arrives, we often think of what we might do differently during the coming year, and sometimes we make resolutions, hoping for better results.

Care partners for loved ones living with dementia know that the stress and the demands on our time will probably not change in the coming year. For some, it may become even more difficult, which is good reason to assess our situation to see if we can do things a little better, a little smarter, and a little easier for ourselves.

So, let me suggest a few New Year resolutions for care partners:

> *Resolve to be kind to yourself!* Remind yourself daily that you are doing the best you can for the person you love. Don't beat yourself up for what you are not able to do.
> *Resolve to create or improve your support network or care-giving team!* Find those people who may bring you meals, shop for you, assist you with household tasks, and offer you respite.
> *Resolve to delegate!* Make a list of your daily tasks and be ready to hand off tasks – no matter how small -- when someone

asks if there is anything they can do to help.

Resolve to attend support groups! Find a group that you are comfortable with so that you may be able to learn from others who share this journey.

Resolve to take care of yourself! - You cannot be a good care partner if you do not take care of yourself. Keep your doctor's appointments, meditate, go for walks, listen to music, read, journal, and take naps. Take time for yourself every day.

Resolve to be social with your person with dementia! Find social activities that you both can take part in, such as memory cafes, community center events, or church socials.

Resolve to continue your education! To properly care for your loved one, you need to understand the disease. Attend workshops, continue to read, look for webinars and videos on line. TeepaSnow.com is a great source for this information.

Resolve to keep up with your journaling! Keeping a journal is therapeutic, and it will help you identify the patterns and routines that will make your task easier.

Resolve to create realistic expectations! You may need to lower your expectations. Don't demand too much from your loved one living with dementia, or too much from yourself.

Resolve to pay attention to what is around you! Your loved one living with dementia requires a calm, predictable, managed environment. Music is one of the best ways to achieve this. Remember to play the music your person loves more often.

Resolve to keep up with your paperwork! Be sure this year that your advanced directives, DNR, living will, and other critical documents are in order. This is the task we too frequently put off until later.

Resolve to be empathetic and practice compassionate care! Just keep reminding yourself: Your loved one is not trying to *give you* a hard time. Your loved one is *having* a hard time. Yes, this is hard for you, but remember that it is even harder for them.

As a former care partner for my husband Albert, I understand that the demands can be overwhelming and all-consuming. I too had to ask for help, and sometimes it was way too late because I thought it was my duty to do it myself. This is a common mistake we can all avoid.

In the coming year, just allow yourself to be open to trying something new. Keep an open mind and look for opportunities to involve others. Try not to focus on the deficits of your loved one living with dementia, but explore what they *can* do to participate with you in their care. Give them a purpose, and find ways to become a *care partner* rather than a caregiver. Care partners often do things *to* and *for* their loved one. This is okay, but it is better to find ways to do things *with* them.

As you make your list of resolutions, remember that they should all be based on an underlying philosophy which I express in my favorite slogan: *We all deserve the best!*

Chapter 37
Dementia is no longer
in the shadows

Since my husband Albert died of dementia in 2010, we have seen significant changes in how our society understands and responds to Alzheimer's disease and other forms of dementia.

During my care partner experience, I could find few people who were willing to even talk about the disease, much less tell me where I could get the information and the support I needed. The most useful thing my family doctor could tell me when Albert was diagnosed was, "Hang on for the ride!" I really resented that lack of help at the time, but now realize there wasn't much more he could tell me.

As with any disease, before we can develop useful knowledge and resources, we must have public awareness and acceptance of our situation on a national scale. Until recently, that public conversation did not exist for dementia. Too often, people with dementia were treated as a family's shame and shoved off into the shadows. Whether we intended to or not, in our ignorance we blamed the victim, making their plight even more terrible than it already was.

I am so happy to note that the state of Alzheimer's Awareness has greatly improved. Not only is it acceptable to discuss the disease, but it is now approaching the status of a topic of great interest in popular culture. Let me give some examples.

This year, two major publications offering a fairly comprehensive knowledge of Alzheimer's disease have appeared on supermarket newsstands. These are "Alzheimer's: New Hope for a Cure" by Centennial Media LLC, and "The Science of Alzheimer's" by Time Inc. Books. Both are priced at about $13.00, and though they may be mixed among the more frivolous tabloids that tell you about the squabbles of the royal family or who Brad Pitt is dating, they are far more substantial publications that deserve to be kept in one's permanent library. And neither contains advertising.

The struggles of families experiencing dementia have also more frequently become the driver of dramatic plots for nationally-distributed movies. After "The Notebook" and "Still Alice" broke ground ten years ago, more recently we saw the Glen Campbell documentary "I'll be Me" followed by "The Judge." Last year brought us "The Leisure Seeker," and this year's release about a family struggling with dementia is "What They Had."

In fact, popular culture has embraced the topic of dementia to the extent that we now see dramatic art forms as diverse as high opera and soap opera tackling the issue. Last summer, Opera Philadelphia presented "Sky on Swings," and for some time now one of America's longest running daytime dramas, the Sentinel Award-winning "General Hospital," has included an Alzheimer's story line.

This increase in the national conversation about dementia is good for several reasons. First, we need to remove any stigma from the topic of dementia for the benefit of those living with the disease, and their families. None of these chose this difficult path, nor should any be ostracized or isolated from society because of it. Though there is currently no cure or remediation for this fatal disease, those living with it deserve the best quality of life for as long as possible, and this requires public acceptance and understanding.

Second, if we are ever going to find medical solutions, including better-funded quality care, a public conversation is required. Political action always follows public demand, so we will never have the funding and support for the resources we need until the public demands it. Our government representatives need to realize and be constantly reminded that dementia is no longer a "minority" issue.

I believe we are moving in the right direction because the greatest segment of our population – the Baby Boomers – has reached the time of life most affected by dementia. Ten percent of this huge generation will get some form of dementia, and I have no doubt that they and their families will demand a greater allocation of public resources to deal with this long and expensive disease.

Let's keep this conversation going. Even if we never find a cure for Alzheimer's, it is our moral and social obligation to provide the best quality of life possible for the individuals and families living with dementia. This is because *We all deserve the best.*

Chapter 38:
The presence and process of grief

Grief is a natural response to a loss of any kind. People associate grief with the death of a loved one, but we can experience grief at many other times in our lives, and for different kinds of loss, both great and small. The collapse of a relationship; the loss of a job; our children leaving the nest; the loss of a pet; all of these can bring us to a state of grief.

There are so many exhausting challenges in caring for a loved one living with dementia, and one of these is the reoccurrence of grief. In my experience, for the family care partner, grief comes again and again. It is the nature of dementia that the person's personality may change again and again during the journey. While you can still recognize the physical person, they have become different with each change. As you lose the person you knew, each discernable change becomes a reason to grieve.

Sadly, this is not a disease that lets us hold off and prepare ourselves for that one big period of grief that begins at the time of our loved one's death. As care partners for individuals living with dementia, we must mentally and emotionally prepare ourselves for a difficult path of recurring grief.

I will tell you from my experience, and from the many conversations I have had with experts in this field, it is very dangerous to try to ignore grief or to try to handle it alone. Most of us simply don't have the energy, specialized knowledge, or life experience to go it alone, and we can permanently damage our ability to function and survive if we try.

Grief is nothing to be ashamed of, and it is definitely not a unique or solitary experience. We all go through it, and the path forward will move more quickly if we accept help, or if we work through it with others who are grieving too. I attended group and solo grief counseling for many months following the death of my husband Albert.

At that time, I could not guess that my future would involve trying to help other care partners for loved ones living with dementia. I was exhausted, I had been cheated by this awful disease, and I was simply done with it! But today it has become my purpose and profession, and I believe this would not have been possible without my being guided through my period of grief by an experienced professional who helped me realize that my trial was a valuable lesson, not just a bitter loss.

Fortunately, in Citrus County there are resources ready and willing to help us through our grief. Most readers will be aware that over the last year we have seen a restructuring of hospice services in our county, and I, for one, was afraid we might lose those bereavement services that had been so valuable to me.

Fortunately, I was wrong. Not only do we still have two hospice organizations to serve us, but from this restructuring emerged an autonomous charitable organization to provide bereavement support along with other valuable services. Its name is Friends of Citrus and the Nature Coast. This is a long name, so let me just call it "Friends" for the remainder of this column.

Its bereavement services include grief support workshops, telephone support, educational materials for parents and teachers, Herry's Kids programs with Camp Good Hope and Teen Encounter (Grief Support Camps), and L.I.F.T. social support for widows and widowers. And many of these services are open to anyone who has experienced loss of any kind, and they have professionals prepared to help you work through it.

Part of working through grief is trying to maintain our sociability, and Friends has programs to help with this as well. For example, they show free classic and recent-release movies at several locations throughout the county.

Friends also offers the Five Wishes Program which helps one conduct the end-of-life planning that we often don't think about until we are faced with a crisis. They also offer Alzheimer's 1 and Alzheimer's 2 classes with state-approved certification that provide valuable knowledge for the care partner or anyone who would like a better understanding of the disease.

As I said above, Friends has emerged as an autonomous organization due to the restructuring of hospice services in Citrus County, but they are actually the same organization that got me through my crisis with the same services and some of the same expert personnel.

There is absolutely no reason to grieve alone. I urge you to take advantage of the support available to you. For information about services or to donate, call 352-249-1470 or 352-454-0844 or visit www.friendsofcitrus.org or Friends of Citrus on Facebook.

Chapter 39:
The Rules of Engagement

Those of us caring for a loved one with dementia know that it is more art than science. What works one day does not the next. There are some basic rules of engagement, but most of the time we must be flexible and creative in dealing with a person who is in a frequent state of change.

The basic rules of engagement involve approach, voice, and touch. We must be mindful of the basic sensory deficits in a person living with dementia. We must remember that their vision has changed; they have reduced peripheral vision and possibly a loss of depth perception. We must remember that their auditory perception has changed as well. They may be experiencing a constant distraction of white noise, they may hear loud and confusing phantom noises, and they will have lost their ability to immediately identify the direction from which a sound is coming.

In addition to their loss of sensory abilities, they will have lost the ability to process information as quickly as we can. What we grasp in an instant may take them several seconds to process, if at all. When we speak at a normal rate, they may completely lose some of the words in the sentence we have spoken.

When we try to be as clear as we can, it may not make sense to them.

We must remember the sensory and cognitive deficits when we approach a person with dementia. The basic rules are: Approach at eye level. Pause more than three feet away to get their attention. Smile, speak slowly, lower your tone of voice, and use simple sentences that contain only one thought or instruction.

Do not approach closer until you have eye contact and an indication that they are ready to receive you. This welcoming indication may be their outstretched hand or a smile. Only then can you approach closer and make physical contact by gently but firmly grasping their dominant hand, which is the hand they might hit with if an improper approach has frightened them.

Never approach quickly or from the side or behind, which will be out of their range of vision. Always use a soothing voice, smile, a compliment, and address them by name. Never use baby-talk; they are adults! Tell them how good they look today or how happy you are to see them. Remember that even when they understand every word you say, they will process the information at a much slower rate. Pause between sentences and never hurry them.

Once you have mastered the skills of approach, voice, and touch, you need to be mindful that their reality may not be the same as yours. Often, a person with dementia may move within their mind to an earlier time in their life. I know a man whose mother started calling him by the name of her brother; his uncle, who had died years ago. This upset him at first, but soon he realized that his mother had moved to a different reality, and he began to work with her within that reality. When she called him by his uncle's name, he responded to it and asked her to talk about the things they liked to do together. The woman described events of decades before, which seemed to make her very happy and put her at ease.

The first time a loved one with dementia does not recognize you or calls you by someone else's name, it really hurts. You must not take it personally; they are not trying to hurt you. You must try to remember that they are not giving you a hard time; they are having a hard time.

The cardinal rule of dementia care is to validate what your loved one believes and says. Never contradict and never argue. You will never be successful in dragging them back into your reality; rather, it is your job to try to understand their reality and validate – not challenge or contradict – their beliefs.

As I said at the outset of this column, effectively engaging your loved one with dementia is an art, not a science. Beyond the basic rules of approach, voice, and touch, you are often in unknown territory. What worked one day may not the next. But if you find ways to validate what they do and say, care-giving will become much easier.

Keep in mind that individuals living with dementia do not live in a world of logic or real time. They live in a world of feelings. They react to how others make them feel. As a care partner, a big part of your job is to make them feel validated and useful. Don't treat them like a task. Treat them like a person of value who may see the world differently than you do, and who is certainly struggling to cope within the world in which you live.

It is never easy, but often when we think they are making it hard on us, it is because we have unintentionally made it hard on them by not understanding and practicing the basic rules of engagement. We need to recognize they see things differently because *We all deserve the best.*

Chapter 40:
Doula: Spiritual support at the end of life

The most undeniable fact of life is that it will end. However, too often families and care partners go to extraordinary lengths to avoid end-of-life planning until it is too late. I have already written about hospice and bereavement counseling as valuable services to care partners coping with dementia. Another is doula.

Doula is a Greek word that means "servant." For centuries, doulas have served as mid-wife assistants, providers, and supporters to women bringing life into the world. End-of-life doulas, which are a more recent phenomenon, are individuals trained and certified to help support and guide individuals and their loved ones through the death and dying process.

Doulas will become more important in a society where our aged population (65 and older) is expected to grow from the current 75 million to 92 million by 2060! Furthermore, 20 percent of the members of this growing population have no children, which further necessitates their reliance on outside support.

Here are some of the services doulas provide:

They educate in the natural end-of-life processes, a knowledge that too many of us carefully but unwisely avoid.

They provide respite care, allowing needed rest and recuperation for care partners and their families.

They provide a compassionate presence throughout the dying process.

They provide assistance with funeral arrangements, obituaries, memorials, and locating bereavement resources.

They work with providers and family members to face end-of-life issues and develop plans on a timely basis so they will not be caught up in disagreements at a time of crisis when they are least able to make critical and rational decisions.

In short, they provide palliative care to assure the best possible quality of life at the most critical moment in our existence.

They can also provide after-death counseling to help loved ones and families get their lives back on track.

Doula is not competitive with hospice. They each provide valuable services and support, and I would never suggest that one is more important than the other. Typically, hospice follows a medical model; doula follows a spiritual model, and a client can benefit from both. Doulas are not nurses, nurse assistants, or social workers, though some doulas may also carry those credentials.

While much of doula work is with families and their care providers, they also are trained in the skills needed to communicate and support the dying. In respect to individuals living with dementia, this requires special skills since that person quite often lacks the ability to think rationally or respond verbally. In these cases, doulas use music, verbal reassurance, and compassionate touch to communicate with a person living with dementia. In this way, they work with a person's feelings rather than rational thought processes.

Saundra Piercy is a doula in the Florida Nature Coast region. About working with individuals living with dementia, she said, "We must create a relationship of the heart. We know that those living in the late stages of dementia still have feelings, and by reaching them on a feeling level, we can contribute to their quality of life." She added, "These techniques can also be taught to their care partners and families; they are simple and basic techniques of kindness, loving voice, and compassionate touch."

Reminding us that doula is for all – not just those living with dementia – Saundra continued, "Our task with the dying is to be fully present; to hold their hand, to touch, to talk, to play the music we know they love. Families often find this difficult, so we can model this role for them, or even share this task with them."

To learn more about doula, go to www.doulagivers.com or to https://www.inelda.org/.

I always end my column by reminding that *We All Deserve the Best."* This is true also at the end of life, perhaps more so than any other time.

Chapter 41:
Can Lyme Disease
cause Alzheimer's?

Lyme is a bacterial disease carried by ticks, transmitted to people through infected blood. With the arrival of summer, we always see more in the news about Lyme. Recently, I have heard a lot of speculation about whether Lyme – or tick bites – might be one of the causes of Alzheimer's disease.

This is an unwarranted concern that I think was caused in part by recent stories about celebrity Kris Kristofferson being diagnosed with Alzheimer's. Recently, it was announced that Kristofferson does not have Alzheimer's, but actually has Lyme, which went misdiagnosed for many years! But this news linked Lyme and Alzheimer's in the popular media, leading to fear and unjustified concern.

Most of the symptoms of Lyme have little resemblance to the symptoms of any kind of dementia, including Alzheimer's. One symptom of Lyme infection is a rash, appearing at the site of the tick bite. It is often ignored because it is not itchy or painful. People may also experience fever and chills, fatigue, muscle or joint pain, and headaches, which can be misdiagnosed as flu.

The misdiagnosis of Lyme can lead to neglect and lack of treatment until more frightening symptoms appear. These can include loss of short-term memory, difficulty in finding common words, and inability to concentrate, causing Lyme to be confused with dementia. This was the case with Kristofferson. But unlike dementia, which is irreversible, Lyme is treatable.

A recent study at the University of Mississauga in Canada has confirmed that there is no link between Lyme and Alzheimer's. This is borne out statistically by the fact that the 13 states in the U.S. with the highest incidence of Lyme disease actually report the lowest number of deaths due to Alzheimer's.

Last month, the American Association of Retired Persons published a survey that indicates that Alzheimer's is our most feared disease among seniors. We need to remind ourselves that 90 percent of us over the age of 65 will *not* get Alzheimer's, and not give ourselves over to fear and panic every time we read new speculation about what causes Alzheimer's and other forms of dementia.

One of these frightening speculations we can put to bed now is that Lyme Disease causes Alzheimer's. It does not!

Chapter 42:
Dementia requires compassionate care

We all have heard of the Hippocratic Oath. It is the code of professional conduct recognized by physicians that dates back to ancient Greece.

The Hippocratic Oath has been revised from time to time, usually in response to medical advances. The Modern Hippocratic Oath contains a sentence that I believe describes how we can care for loved ones living with dementia. It states:

"I will remember that there is art to medicine as well as science, and that warmth, sympathy, and understanding may outweigh the surgeon's knife or the chemist's drug."

To date, dementia has defied the surgeon's knife and the chemist's drug. It is progressive, irreversible, and fatal; and despite the millions we have spent to find a cure, we still have no medical technology that will cure Alzheimer's and other dementias.

Until we can find a cure, we have only one recourse, which is care. Dementia, I believe requires a special kind of care that I call Compassionate Care.

Again, we return to Ancient Greece to understand what we mean by "Compassionate Care." Compassion is not pity, and it is more than sympathy. In classical Greek, the word means "to suffer with" or "suffering together." This graphically describes how we must become attuned to the feelings and needs of our loved ones with dementia in order to give them effective care.

The foundation of Compassionate Care is the knowledge that even in the final stages of dementia, a person does not lose the ability to experience emotions. This means emotion is ultimately the only way we can connect with them.

We can do this through loving voice and touch, through hug therapy, through validation of their feelings, and with music. And, as the Hippocratic Oath suggests, this level of medical care is art, not science. It takes practice, experience, courage, and inspiration.

We must practice Compassionate Care for the benefit of our loved one, but we do it also for ourselves. It can make the difficult journey more rewarding and fulfilling for both of us, and *We both deserve the best.*

Chapter 43:
Beware bogus brain boosters

According to the American Association of Retired Persons, one in four over the age of 50 takes a brain supplement, despite the fact that they are likely only flushing their money down the drain!

Why would we do this? Sadly, because opportunists in the darker corners of our health care industry prey on our fear and misunderstanding about Alzheimer's disease and other causes of dementia. When asked what disease seniors fear most, respondents to an AARP survey named Alzheimer's disease their greatest fear. As a cause for concern, it ranks above cancer, stroke, and heart disease, in that order. As a result, many readily buy supplements, pills, and other products that falsely claim to improve and protect our brain.

This is no small problem. These products amount to a $3 billion-dollar industry according to a study conducted by the AARP Global Council on Brain Health, and this expenditure is expected to double by 2023 as our senior population continues to grow. The study concluded that "scientific evidence does not support the use of any supplement to prevent, slow, reverse, or stop cognitive decline, dementia, or other related neurological disease such as Alzheimer's," and that use of such products is a "massive waste of money."

In addition, these products do not fall under the laws that regulate our prescription medications. No federal agency tests supplements and herbal remedies through clinical trials, verifies that they meet medical claims, or certifies their purity or dosage. All we know about them is what their manufacturers and marketers tell us, and, according to the AARP, it is simply not to be believed.

We all deserve the best, which bogus brain boosters are not!

Chapter 44:
Nostalgia Therapy

There is still so much we do not know about what is happening in the minds of persons living with dementia. Why do they seem to sometimes get so far afield from reality?

We, as the people presumably in touch with reality, see their thinking as flawed, fictional, and delusional. We are troubled when they believe things that are just not *real* or *never happened*. I would suggest that in order to be a good care partner, this is a point of view from which we must step away.

One thing we do know is that short term memory is the first to degrade with the onset of most dementias. Then the loss of memory often moves backward until they lose recollection of huge segments of their life.

But we see remarkable exceptions to this rule. Sometimes, people with dementia retain vivid memories of earlier times. Their current reality becomes a version of an earlier time in their life.

When this happens, it should be considered a blessing and a useful tool for better care; not a troubling delusion. This is an opportunity to better bond by meeting them in *their reality.*

Even for those of us of sound mind, nostalgia is often not accurate to the way things really were. We filter out the bad and focus on the things we enjoyed about the past, and we create our own "Good Old Days." I wonder how different this is from a person living with dementia.

By accepting rather than discounting "dementia reality," a new practice called Nostalgia Therapy has emerged. Memory Care facilities are beginning to decorate their rooms with artifacts from the era when their residents were young.   I know of one facility that actually had a 1956 Chevy in its building!

We are seeing new senior day care facilities that look like a 1950s town, complete with diner, movie theater (that shows old films), and old-style hardware or drug stores. Seniors, with and without dementia, enjoy this environment.

Nostalgia Therapy works, and I think it can lead us to even greater understanding and acceptance of what is going on in the mind of a loved one living with dementia.

So, the next time a person with dementia tells you something you know to be entirely untrue; don't argue, just listen. Don't refute their beliefs; explore them. And when your mother mistakes you for her long-gone sister, don't get your ego in a twist. Rather, smile and consider the idea that maybe she has recognized you as someone in her life that she dearly loved and is happy to see again.

Chapter 45:
We need both Cure and Care

A survey conducted recently by the American Association of Retired Persons reconfirmed that Alzheimer's and other forms of dementia are our most feared disease; significantly more feared than cancer, heart attack, and stroke. This would explain why people are so willing to give generously to research for a cure.

While a massive effort to end Alzheimer's is certainly justified, I believe that sometimes our desire to find a cure overshadows our need to focus equally on care. After all, for those nearly six million Americans who are already living with Alzheimer's disease, and the more than 16 million who provide unpaid care, a cure is already too late.

We will be conducting our Third Annual Walk Aware for Alzheimer's in Floral City on the 19th of this month. In its first two years, this Walk has raised more than $50,000 for the Alzheimer's Family Organization, a regional nonprofit that dedicates all of its resources to – not research for a cure – but to caregivers of individuals living with dementia in Citrus, Hernando, Marion, and other west-central Florida counties.

Thanks to volunteers and generous in-kind support from many people, national chains, and local businesses, this Walk's expenses have been held to eight percent of revenue or less, meaning that each year we gave 92 cents or more from each dollar earned to the AFO! Very few fund-raising events can boast this kind of efficiency and return on investment!

While other organizations promote Walks to "end Alz," this Walk's sole purpose is to help those already living with Alzheimer's and other forms of dementia. While we will all continue to hope for that illusive cure, we must also remember that until there is a cure, there is care . . . there is only care!

Chapter 46:
Scent Kits: Safeguard against wandering

November is National Alzheimer's Month, declared so by President Ronald Reagan in 1983. In Citrus County, we have a double observance for our loved ones living with dementia because our Board of County Commissioners has just named November Citrus County Scent Kits for Safety Month as well.

A Scent Kit – short for Human Scent Preservation Kit – is an inexpensive way to collect and retain an individual's unique pure scent, which can be used to reduce the time and increase the success of bloodhounds tracking someone who has wandered and become lost. Creating a Scent Kit is a good idea for everyone, including children, but it is especially important for individuals living with dementia because they are prone to wander.

Scent Kits have proven effective many times in Citrus County, and more than 15,000 have been distributed here. As news of our success has spread, more than 10,000 Scent Kits have been requested by agencies in other counties.

Our kits, branded "Out of Harm's Way Scent Kits," are funded by the non-profit Find-M' Friends, assembled at the Key Training Center, and distributed by several parties that include the Sheriff's Office, our libraries, and my company, Coping with Dementia LLC. Widespread distribution has been possible because Find-M' Friends has learned how to manufacture them for about $2.00 each!

I can brag forever about what we have accomplished in Citrus County with Scent Kits, but what good is this to you if you don't have one for your loved one living with dementia, for yourself, and for others in your family, including your children? Please, take advantage of this inexpensive way to improve your safety and the safety of the ones you love.

Scent Kits . . . because we all deserve the best!

Chapter 47:
Let's build a better Baker Act

If we are going to continue to use the Baker Act as a tool for dementia care, let's do it right!

When the Baker Act was enacted fifty years ago as a new concept to provide safety and services to citizens suffering from mental illness, I doubt that anyone realized the future role it would play in the lives of individuals and families living with dementia. Dementia was not so well understood at that time, and a combination of longer life span and population growth over the past five decades has brought it to the fore, causing the Baker Act – whether intended or not – to become the place where dementia and mental illness intersect.

My own experience with the care of my husband Albert, who was twice Baker Acted due to his "dementia behavior," was horrific, and my hope is that we will fashion a future where this will not happen to others. My perfect world would provide that our loved ones living with dementia never be Baker Acted, but I suspect this is not realistic.

I do not challenge the letter or intent of this law, but I believe there are provisions we can make in its implementation that will make it more acceptable, and hopefully even helpful, for families living with dementia. These provisions involve relatively simple and inexpensive aspects of facility design and staff training.

First, I believe individuals living with dementia should never be admitted into a general population where noise, aggressive behavior, and over-stimulation is likely to cause them greater emotional stress and possibly physical injury. My husband was sent back to me beaten and bruised. I do not suggest the staff did this, but I know that he was placed among other people who did not have dementia and were there for violent and dangerous behavior.

Our Baker Act facility should have segregated screening, admission, and holding procedures for individuals living with dementia, including those of a senior age who are likely to have dementia. These holding areas should be separate from loud noise sources and even, if possible, include soothing and tranquil music. They should be designed to not look like jail cells, and be painted in soothing colors. And, they should be managed by staff who have been trained in the causes of so-called "dementia behaviors," and how to interpret and respond appropriately and compassionately.

This approach is not new. In 2018. shortly after Citrus County adopted LifeStream Behavioral Services as its mental health provider, I had the opportunity to tour its Baker Act facility in Leesburg, and I was delighted to see that it was following a policy to segregated admission and treatment for individuals with dementia. Our county government should insist that this policy be followed in our new Citrus County facility.

The second critical component is training, which will not be as expensive and time-consuming as one might believe. Staff at our Baker Act facility, and the first responders who provide transportation for those being Baker Acted, should receive dementia-specific training. I believe this can be accomplished through a two-hour session for care staff, and a one-hour orientation for first responders. This training will include an explanation of what causes the so-called "dementia behaviors," how to interpret those behaviors, and how to respond appropriately, compassionately, and effectively.

How the Baker Act is initiated should be refined. Regrettably, the process is initiated too often from professional care facilities, which should have the training to rely on de-escalation, rather than removal. If a memory care facility builds a record for frequent use of the Baker Act, the Agency for Health Care Administration should move in and require remedial training of its management and care staff.

When law enforcement is called to initiate the Baker Act, a gentler approach should be used. Recent experiments in Denver and other cities have proven that the need to forcibly remove people is greatly reduced when the Baker Act team – not wearing police uniforms -- arrives in an ambulance or an unmarked car, rather than a police cruiser. With this gentler approach, the de-escalation rate rises and the removal rate significantly declines.

We need follow-up and education for the public. Baker acts are usually initiated in an atmosphere of fear and panic, and most of the families who initiate the process have no idea where it will lead or how damaging it can be to their person with dementia and their relationship with that person.

So, let's deal with it at the source. Families that have initiated a Baker Act should be offered after-the-fact counseling and training so they can be given knowledge of alternatives for action that will avoid their doing it a second time.

There are an estimated 6,500 individuals in Citrus County living with dementia today. This number is projected to grow to more than 15,000 by 2050. How we treat our loved ones living with dementia is going to become an ever-growing component in our county's overall quality of life.

We are at the threshold of a wonderful opportunity to make Citrus County a model for compassionate and enlightened treatment for individuals living with dementia – and their families – in our new Baker Act facility and procedure. Let us seize and make the best of this opportunity!

We should have a better Baker Act process and facility because we all deserve the best!

Chapter 48:
Dementia and Firearm Safety

You would be surprised how often I hear from concerned care partners for loved ones living with dementia who have open access to firearms. Unfortunately, gun ownership is like so many aspects of living with dementia; we often don't think much about it until we are confronted with a crisis.

Dementia erodes good judgment, reduces cognition, slows reflexes, and impairs the senses, including vision, hearing, manual dexterity, and fine motor skills. In short, dementia attacks every ability we need to safely handle firearms.

Let me interject here that we are not embarking on an argument against gun ownership. Firearms may become more dangerous in a home where someone is living with dementia, but the same thing can be said for automobiles, knives, electrical appliances, and household chemicals.

Whether it is a firearm or something else, in every case it comes down to two simple words: "awareness" and "planning." But immediacy is in order. Putting it off until a crisis arises is not planning! And ignoring a potential problem can be fatal.

Fortunately, there is a Florida nonprofit called Dementia Education Inc. that has just published a new booklet entitled "Dementia and Firearm Safety." It contains writings by a variety of experts that includes Certified Dementia Practitioners, an attorney who specializes in Gun Trusts, an award-winning target shooter who has made firearms safety a family affair, a retired law enforcement officer, and a licensed firearms dealer. Their collective knowledge is brought together to suggest a variety of ways you and your loved one with dementia can plan to remain safe. "Dementia and Firearm Safety" is available at Amazon for $9.95.

If you own firearms and are caring for a loved one living with dementia; start your planning now! Don't wait until you are confronted with a dangerous and possibly lethal situation.

Chapter 49:
Going to their world

I often hear care partners express anger, frustration, or sadness that their loved one living with dementia seems to be in another world. They may believe they are living in another time, or different place. They may forget your name or call you by the name of someone else they have known.

Rather than argue or correct their mistaken beliefs, we must put our own reality – and sometimes our own egos – aside to go to and accept their world, as hard as this may seem.

Admittedly, it is a painful moment when a family member you have known your whole life calls you by another name; but your correcting or arguing is not going to change their thinking. It only risks angering them, hurting their feelings, and eroding their trust.

When this clash of realities happens, the first thing we must do is take a deep breath, step back emotionally, and remind ourselves: "They are not trying to give me a hard time! They are having a hard time!"

It will not help to tell them they are wrong. This only hardens the boundaries between your reality and their reality. Rather, remind yourself that what they believe, though not factual or accurate, is their reality, and as valid for them as your reality is for you.

In these challenging moments, we must remember the first rule of dementia care: Don't argue, ever, about anything! Rather, avoid confrontation and look for opportunities to validate what they believe, even though it may not match your version of the truth.

For example, don't say, "I'm not your brother; I'm your son!" Instead, try something like, "Thank you. I know you've always loved me, and I love you." This keeps the issue of your identity entirely out of the discussion, but it tells your loved one you feel good about what they have said.

Care partners may find this acceptance of their loved one's "mistaken" reality painful at first, but as you see beneficial results, you will begin to find it easier to go to their world. Validation eliminates points of conflict and reduces anxiety for both you and your loved one with dementia. It proves you are listening to them and that you understand their beliefs are important to them.

Like practically every aspect of dementia care, it is not always easy to do. But it gets easier with practice and patience. Don't think of it as abandoning your own reality. Think of it as expanding your reality to bring the two of you into a world of better communication and mutual respect.

I can tell you from my own experience, when you learn to enter their world without judgment, you will discover some beautiful ideas and feelings that make it easier to replace conflict with compassion. It is a way to fulfill your belief that you both deserve the best!

Chapter 50:
Sociability can improve quality of life

We had two very special speakers at our recent Coping with Dementia Family Care Partner Conference. No, they were not experts in brain science telling us that a cure for Alzheimer's is just around the corner.   Nor were they health professionals claiming that herbs and supplements can reverse dementia.

They were two men who have lived with a dementia diagnosis for ten years, speaking eloquently about their quality of life!

Just a few years ago, Daniel Jamieson was delivered to an Inverness memory care facility. His family said he was out of control and that they could no longer manage him. Mr. Jamieson has become that facility's volunteer gardener, skillfully caring for plants both inside and outside the building. He is calm, conversational, and often helps the staff manage other residents living with dementia.

Earl Mills is a musician who plays guitar and sings . . . from memory! He opened our conference with a stirring acapella rendition of "America the Beautiful," bringing many in the audience to tears.

When these two remarkable men had an opportunity to speak to 200 people, they did not talk about the pain and suffering of dementia. They did not even talk about how their special talents – horticulture and music – benefit them. Rather, they talked about the satisfaction it gives them to bring joy to others with what they still can do!

Too often, our reaction to a diagnosis of dementia is to throw up our hands in despair and give up to the disease. I believe that sometimes our attitude toward dementia is as damaging as the disease itself.

Even with dementia, we have the opportunity to focus on and nurture the talents, skills, and abilities that remain, and by emphasizing the positive we can bring joy and a continuing quality of life to our loved ones, ourselves, and the many others we meet during the process of managing dementia.

We must stop thinking of a dementia diagnosis as a death sentence. We must remember that even under difficult circumstances, sociability is a powerful tool. By seeking out and pursuing the opportunities to remain social and active, we can achieve a better quality of life for ourselves and our loved ones living with dementia. This is a fact for which Mr. Mills and Mr. Jamieson are living proof. Daniel and Earl, we thank you for reminding us! You have shown us that – whether or not we have been diagnosed with dementia – we all deserve the best!

Chapter 51:
Use Simple Therapies
That Trigger Good Feelings

Medicine today is so driven by technology and pharmacology, we too often overlook the ways we can ease pain and improve quality of life through simple therapies based on love, compassion, respect, and dignity.

The field of dementia care is an area where compassion can get better results than the use of drugs. This is because the organs in our brain that govern our emotions – the amygdala – survive and continue to function long after dementia has ravaged the "thinking" parts of our brain.

Consequently, the "feeling" part of our brain can be the last and only tool a care partner has to work with. We can do this with simple therapies that have been known and used for decades; in some cases, even for centuries. They include:

Nostalgia Therapy – It is not uncommon for individuals living with dementia to lose their recent memories, yet be able to retain recollection of an earlier time in their life. Sometimes, they "go there" and seem to live in that earlier time. This should not be dismissed as "delusional;" rather it should be recognized as a valuable tool for effective and compassionate care. Use nostalgic artifacts and reminiscence about their past life to validate the reality that seems to give them comfort.

Hug Therapy – Hugs are proven to work, especially for people living with brain disorders, but many of our care partners don't practice it enough. I saw it work with my husband Albert, so effectively that he was removed entirely from mood-altering medication.

Music Therapy – Music Therapy is another proven non-pharmacological therapy that can work wonders. Similar to Nostalgia Therapy, it seems to work best when we choose music that our loved one enjoyed between the ages of eight and 20. To see just how effective it is, go to YouTube and watch "Alive Inside."

Doll Therapy – Many times, a soft doll will become the constant companion of a person living with dementia, especially women. It seems to give them comfort and a sense of purpose. Some people think an older person holding a doll is "demeaning." I don't agree. If it gives your loved one comfort, it is not demeaning. There's a lesson here. We, as care partners, must sometimes put our own opinions and feelings aside in favor of how something makes our loved one feel.

Animal Therapy – No need to say much about this! Who doesn't love a puppy or a kitten? Many memory care communities maintain "house pets" because they know how much their residents enjoy and love them. And "animal therapy" works just as well with animatronic pets. These are battery-powered "robots" that behave realistically. People with dementia don't seem to have the slightest concern that they are "not real."

Plant Therapy – Even people in later stages of dementia can love the beauty of plants. However, if they are able, you may want to ask your person to help you tend your plants. Sure, they may make a little mess, but working in soil can give them long periods of joy and comfort.

These and other simple and time-tested therapies are very effective for individuals living with dementia. This is because, long after they seem to have lost the ability to think and reason, they still retain the ability to "feel." And it is our job as care partners to help them create and retain these good feelings because we all deserve the best.

Chapter 52:
The up-side of adversity

Many years ago, I told someone I had a problem, and she said, "No, you have an opportunity." I thought this was just a silly platitude, but over the years, I began to understand what she meant. Every event has positive and negative aspects, and it is we who choose which way we are going to look at it.

Social distancing during the COVID-19 crisis simply destroyed my "normal" way of doing things when every workshop, speaking engagement, and support group from early March through mid-May of 2019 was canceled. And we remained "closed" for the remainder of the year and into 2020! It happened to all of us.

My partner Ed and I used up nearly two weeks doing projects around the house, then we realized we really needed to get back to work. We started looking for the opportunity in our problem, and realized we needed to find a different way of working with our dementia care partners. I have always resisted video technology for educating and consulting because it seemed so distant and impersonal, but now it seemed to be the only option.

We were finally kicked into action when my friend Linda Burhans, the creator and host of the Connecting Caregivers Radio Show, called and asked, "Have you ever done your support groups on line?" She too was looking for the opportunity in her problem, which was similar to ours.

Not only did Linda's call help me decide to take the on-line plunge, but we also decided to team up as co-facilitators on a series of on-line support groups using the Zoom internet service.

What an eye-opener this experience has been! It is definitely different from meeting with a group in person, but that "distance" and "impersonal" quality I was so concerned about has just not happened. Our first on-line support groups have been warm, meaningful, fun, and even joyful.

And they have provided outreach and connection that were previously not possible. For example, the first meeting Linda and I facilitated had our usual core of central Florida care partners, but people also joined us from Washington state, Ohio, and Ontario, Canada!

Ironically, all I needed to discover this new opportunity was to take the advice I give care partners every day of the week. When they struggle with loved ones whose personalities and behaviors are changing due to dementia, I often say, "You have to try something! Your situation has changed. Your old responses and behaviors will no longer work. Try something new!"

E-mail or call me to learn about how to join our on-line dementia care partner support groups. Do it because we all deserve the best! They're free!

Chapter 53:
COVID-19 has changed
the conversation

When social distancing began in response to COVID-19, I, and other dementia practitioners, could no longer facilitate support groups for the care partners of individuals living with Alzheimer's and other forms of dementia.

Previously, I had conducted two on-site support groups per month, but these had to be canceled and hastily reorganized as virtual meetings through on-line technology. With workshops, speaking engagements, and other face-to-face events also canceled, I suddenly had more time and more demand for on-line contact, and soon I found myself facilitating as many as ten on-line meetings a month. And with no geographical limitations, we've had people joining us from as far away as Oregon and Ontario!

So, clearly, COVID-19 has revolutionized the methodology and frequency of care partner support meetings. But what I did not anticipate was that it would also significantly change the nature of the conversation by confronting each of us with the question, "What will happen to my loved one with dementia if I suddenly become incapacitated?"

Typically, support groups dedicate a lot of time to the *crisis-du-jour*; the problems caused by their loved one's behavior that they do not know how to cope with. Usually, this leaves little time to talk about the care partner's health and wellbeing, or for contingency planning in the event that they too become ill or incapacitated.

I now see among my support groups a keen interest in discussing the issues that are inevitable but not yet pressing. These include conversations about powers-of-attorney, healthcare surrogacy, professional placement, financial planning, arranging for third-party support, and – perhaps the most important of all -- self-care! Let's face it; if we don't take care of ourselves and prudently plan, one day there may be no one to take care of our loved one with dementia.

So COVID-19 has definitely flipped the agenda. While crisis management is still, and always will be, an important issue, there is now a greater emphasis on contingency planning. I consider this a healthy trend. More intelligent discussion among care partners about contingency planning today will result in a reduced need for crisis management in the future, and this is a good thing because we both – the care partner and our loved one with dementia – deserve the best.

Chapter 54:
Hurricane season
brings special challenges

Floridians understand how to prepare for seasonal bad weather, but for families living with dementia, hurricane season can present special challenges.

Individuals living with Alzheimer's and other forms of dementia do not have the benefit of memory, so they cannot reassure themselves from the knowledge that most tropical storms do little or no damage. For them, every new harsh weather experience can be terrifying.

Just being moved from their home or community to a strange shelter may be upsetting because it shatters their routine and confronts them with an unfamiliar environment.

Care partners can plan for a weather emergency by creating a kit that contains at least three days of supplies. This kit should be assembled in advance and stored away. Do not try to assemble your kit at the last minute, and especially not in the presence of your loved one, which could cause anxiety and panic.

Know your evacuation route and pre-register at your county's special needs shelter in case you have to evacuate. If possible, staying with a neighbor, family member, or a friend may be a better alternative than a public shelter since your loved one may accept it as a more "normal" environment.

If your loved one lives in a professional care community, become familiar with its disaster and evacuation plan so you will not be faced with last-minute surprises.

As a general rule, plan in advance, stay calm, and look for ways to continue the activities your loved one likes and understands.

For more information, contact the National Institute on Aging which offers an extensive disaster planning toolkit. Go to www.nia.nih/health/disaster-preparedness-alzheimers-caregivers.

The list below should be posted in a safe place for planning purposes.

Emergency Preparedness List

Easy on/off comfortable clothes (a couple of sets)
Easy on/off comfortable shoes/sneakers
Blanket or jacket
Second pair of eye glasses
Incontinence products, wipes
Toiletry supplies for three to four days
Personal identification (ID bracelets, clothing tags)

Human scent preservation kit
Medication and use/dosage information in a
Ziploc bag
Legal documents in a Ziploc bag
List of emergency contact numbers
Recent photo of your loved one with vital
information on the back
Battery operated radio with extra batteries
Flashlight and batteries
Portable music device with earphones to shut
out noise
Simple activities such as cards, photo albums,
scrapbooks, coloring books
Cell phone recharger
Favorite drinks and snacks
A tracking device for your loved one.

And don't forget that we all deserve the best!

Chapter 55:
Time for a Gratitude List

COVID-19 has been tough on all of us. Isolation, fear of infection, and the confusing debate that has gone on over the scientific aspects of the virus are making us crazy! None of us is immune to the negative social impact of our situation, and especially not individuals living with dementia, their families, and their care partners.

Think you have it tough? How would you like it if the only contact with your loved one locked down in a memory care facility is to try to speak to them on a cell phone while waving and smiling through a window? This is emotionally difficult for those of us with unimpaired thinking processes, but imagine how confusing it must be for your loved one who is living with dementia.

The challenges of COVID have been a frequent topic within the care partner support groups I facilitate on line each week. So, recently I began to suggest a technique that I have seen work time and again: Make a Gratitude List, or write a letter of gratitude to someone you know.

"That's it!" you say? "A Gratitude List when everything in my life seems to have gone to hell?"

Yes. In fact, those times when we seem to have the least to be grateful for are the best times to identify and talk about the positive things in our lives. This is not some kind of new-age, rose-colored-glasses mind game. There is real science behind it.

Neuropsychologists have studied the effects of positive thinking for about 20 years now, and time and again the research shows that the active practice of gratitude releases dopamine and serotonin in the brain. These are the chemicals that make us feel good. Not only is it momentarily beneficial, but over time it creates a systemic process where positive thoughts generate these beneficial chemicals, and the beneficial chemicals lead to more positive thoughts that may help you become a better care partner for your individual living with dementia.

World religions have known this for eons. They call it prayer; not the prayer when we ask for what we want, but the prayer when we give thanks for what we have.

Try it. Your first gratitude list may seem hard to do, and it may contain only one or two items. That's okay. When you least expect it, that dopamine and serotonin may kick in, and suddenly your list gets a little longer. The only thing you have to lose is your unhappy thoughts!

Chapter 56:
Because Loneliness kills!

A few years ago, I spoke with a hospice chaplain who said, "You know, I don't believe people die from dementia. I believe people with dementia die from neglect, loneliness, and grief!" I will never forget those words because they so accurately describe the cruelty of this disease.

Late last February, assisted living and memory care facilities began to close to the public, setting in place quarantine systems to keep their residents safe from COVID-19. Suddenly, residents were isolated even from their own families, many of whom previously visited regularly to assist with their care.
Now, more than six months later, we are beginning to witness the cruel outcome of isolation, especially for individuals living with dementia who do not have the cognitive ability to understand why this is happening to them. Many are declining more rapidly than they should, and some are dying alone without the support of their families.

Facilities have tried to compensate with window visits, on-line meetings, and other novel methods of keeping residents in touch with their loved ones. But these are poor substitutes for closeness and real human touch, and for people with dementia they likely create more anxiety and confusion than relief.

When these survival tactics were established, none of us had any idea how long this situation would continue, and now we find ourselves horrified that there appears to be no end in sight.

Something happened in Florida in July that brought this situation into the light of day. A woman named Mary Daniel, like other loved ones, was cut off from her husband who was in a memory care facility, and she could see how badly the isolation was affecting both of them, individually and through their relationship.

Daniel noticed that the staff could come and go, and she applied for a part-time job as a dishwasher. As a result, two days a week, after her shift, she could visit her husband and even lie in bed with him as he went to sleep, just as she had done before COVID.

Daniel's bitter-sweet story struck a chord! The news media picked it up and soon even Florida's governor was talking about her. Daniel grasped on this unexpected publicity to create an organization called Caregivers for Compromise, a grassroots initiative to ask governments and the senior care industry to look for new, compassionate, and humane solutions. Caregivers for Compromise put up a

Facebook page that attracted 6,000 followers in 24 hours! Within two weeks, chapters had formed in every state! Clearly, Mary Daniel was not alone!

The message of Daniel and her group is, if we cannot change COVID, then we must change how our senior care industry responds to it. Why this change is urgent and imperative is expressed in Caregiver for Compromise's motto: "Because isolation kills too!"

This is not a confrontational movement. Daniel has set its tone with the word "comprise." Let's find ways to work with – not against – the professionals and government regulators to make it better for each and all of us. As a result, several states have already begun to review their regulations to address this issue.

COVID has given us another opportunity to learn and improve. I am optimistic that we can come out of this crisis with a more compassionate, more flexible, more creative senior care industry. We definitely should, because we all deserve the best.

Chapter 57:
Watch your Vitamin D

I have a friend who spent a 35-year career in a northern state, and each year struggled with seasonal depression, especially in the gray months of January and February. Once retired, he headed for sunny Florida. It was not just the cold and snow he was tired of. It was those sunless months when his spirits crashed.

A few years after moving to Florida, he was diagnosed with an autoimmune lung disorder, which his doctor has been able to manage with medication. Everything seemed to be going well until this spring when suddenly he became fatigued and began to experience difficulty breathing. He was so tired, there were days he could barely find the strength to get out of bed. Breathing tests and CT scans showed that his lung disease had not progressed, but he felt so bad that he became convinced he was dying.

When time rolled around for routine bloodwork, it was discovered that his Vitamin D level was extremely low. He started a daily Vitamin D supplement, and soon his fatigue was gone, his mood improved, and his breathing eased. He had been experiencing severe depression, but how was this possible in sunny Florida; and why now?

Due to his lung condition, my friend self-isolated to the extreme when COVID-19 arrived last winter, and his new quarantine-based lifestyle had become pretty much "sunless!" When he realized this, his depression suddenly made sense.

I began to think about how quarantine has affected people living with dementia. With memory care and assisted living communities locked down, we are seeing those with dementia decline more rapidly than usual. Isolation, loneliness, and separation from their loved ones is resulting in more rapid loss of weight, verbal skills, cognition, and morale.

I have begun to wonder to what extent Vitamin D deficiency can account for at least part of this decline. Yes, I realize dementia is progressive by nature, but wouldn't it be an interesting and simple solution if we could eliminate at least part of this decline with better attention to Vitamin D?

Low Vitamin D had an extreme effect on my friend – who does not have dementia – and attention to that deficit caused a quick recovery. It leads me to make the simple suggestion that care partners everywhere at least look at this issue and ask for D-level testing. It could result in an improvement in quality of life, and in the absence of a cure, quality of life is the only gift we can give our loved ones living with dementia.

Consider it because we all deserve the best.

Chapter 58:
Let's not scare our care partners!

Providing care for a loved one with dementia is one of the most exhausting care partner tasks there is, because the disease is progressive and ultimately requires attention 24/7.

To drive this message home, speakers about Alzheimer's and dementia – including acknowledged experts – often assert that 70 percent of family care providers die before their loved one with dementia!

I cannot count the times I have heard this claim, in both lectures and casual conversation among people who are trained in this field. It is an apocryphal story that has become deeply woven into the folklore of dementia, but it is simply not true!

Surely, when the experts report this grim but erroneous statistic, they intend to encourage care partners to be more mindful to take care of themselves; to care for their own health as much as that of their loved one. But I fear the result may be the opposite. To tell a group of care partners that 70 percent of them will die before their person with dementia likely only demoralizes them and fills them with even more despair about the grim road ahead, thus pushing their stress levels even higher.

A 2018 study reported by the National Institute of Health concluded, "Although a handful of studies have examined mortality among caregivers of persons with Alzheimer's disease or a related dementia, the proportion of caregivers who die before their cognitively impaired care recipients remains unknown."

In these previous studies, the database was either too small or the conditions too uncontrolled to create reliable results, and none supported the 70 percent claim for caregiver mortality that is so casually thrown around in conversation.

To the contrary, the 2018 NIH study, which is rigorous and based on 17 years of data, found that 18 percent of care partners die before the loved one they are caring for. This means that more than 80 percent of care partners survive their loved one with dementia, which is quite the opposite from the belief that 70 percent of caregivers die first! The referenced study can be found at https://www.ncbi.nlm.nih.gov/pmc/articles/PMC6292823/.

So, I appeal to all in the medical industry and care community to stop telling care partners that they are 70 percent more likely to die first and leave their loved one with dementia behind and alone. Their task is stressful enough, and they don't need to be frightened with unfounded warnings of impending doom.

We want to encourage care partners to seek and welcome help, such as the advice and companionship one can find in a support group. Positive motivation is always better than trying to frighten someone into taking action.

Chapter 59:
Animatronics for joy and comfort

"Animatronics!" Wow, that's a big word! But wait, don't be intimidated. It's simply a modern and high-tech version of something that has always worked so well for our loved ones living with dementia . . . Animal Therapy.

Anyone who has worked in health care knows how much joy and comfort dogs, cats, and other animals can bring to our seniors, whether or not they are living with dementia. This is why a great many assisted living communities have a resident dog or cat.

But what if circumstances won't allow your loved one to own and tend to a live pet? This is when animatronic animals become an option. These are battery-powered, puppet-like dogs or cats that can move and make sounds in response to voice or other outside stimuli.

They range from a sleeping cat or dog that simply breathes, to highly complex models driven by motors, computers, and sensors that are quite realistic. Prices can range from $40 to more than $200, depending on their sophistication.

Let me give you just one example of how they work. One day, just before one of my ABC of

Dementia workshops, a young woman approached and said, "I want to apologize in advance. I have brought my mother who has dementia, and I know she cannot possibly sit through the whole presentation. I will learn what I can, but I am sure we will have to leave before it's over."

I picked up my little breathing cat and said, "May I meet your mother?" I was introduced to her, and I said, "Would you watch my cat Penny during my presentation?" The daughter looked shocked, and whispered to me, "That's not real!" I whispered back, "Maybe to you it's not." In the meantime, mother had broken into a big smile as she took the animatronic cat out of my hands.

Throughout my presentation, the woman sat quietly and gently stroked the soft fur of the little breathing puppet. She remained calm the whole two hours, and after the workshop her daughter said to me in astonishment, "My mother has not sat still that long in her whole life!"

Animatronic pets really work. At my suggestion, many care partners who attend my support groups have acquired one for their loved one living with dementia. They often laugh and joyfully share storied about how much their partners love their little pets.

Animatronic pets do not have to be complex and expensive. As I said, the simple "breathers" seem to be as effective as the more complex and expensive robotic type. They can be acquired on line. Try one. I promise you will be amazed by the joyful response from your loved one living with dementia.

Chapter 60:
How do people
with dementia learn?

Dementia is progressive, irreversible, and ultimately fatal. It attacks all of our senses and abilities, but is best known as a disease that destroys our memory. Typically, it attacks short-term memory first, then begins to erode older memories.

Dementia attacks other mental functions as well, such as cognition, rational thinking skills, and perception of time and space. This makes it impossible for individuals living with dementia to learn by conventional methods.

But I believe our loved ones with dementia are still capable of learning, and I will try to illustrate this from my experience with my husband Albert, who died from dementia.

Albert was treated very badly by "the system." He was kicked out of three assisted living facilities and Baker Acted twice, and in one case returned to me in a taxi, bruised and battered. He was placed in a psychiatric hospital for 12 weeks and held in four-point restraints for seven days!

Finally, a few months before his death, I found a memory care community that handled things quite differently. There, the staff practiced "hug therapy." Every time Joan – the owner – walked into Albert's room, she would smile, hold out her arms, and say, "Good morning, Mr. Albert!" After what Albert had been through, he trusted no one and showed no interest in hugging or being touched in any way.

But about the third day of Albert's residence in this wonderful community, something surprising happened. When Joan walked into the room, Albert suddenly stood up and held out his arms! Albert's relationship with the staff and other residents blossomed. His medications were discontinued and he spent his final days in peace and tranquility.

This was clearly a learning process, but how could a man so deeply damaged by dementia learn? I think the answer lies in understanding two small organs in our brain called the "amygdala," which govern our emotions. The amygdala help us interpret and respond to the things we find both pleasing or painful. What is most wonderful about these organs is that they continue to function long after the rest of the brain has been ravaged by dementia.

Compassionate care is based on the principle that we can manage and provide better quality of life for our loved ones living with dementia through kindness, and understanding their needs by observing their behaviors. When we respond in a way that their amygdala tells them is safe, pleasurable, and trustworthy, they will respond in a positive way.

Communicating through positive emotions is the basis for all compassionate therapies, which include music therapy, pet therapy, hug therapy, and many others. Our loved ones with dementia will respond, not through a rational learning process, but through learning on an emotional level. This is the pathway to a better quality of life for both our care partners and their persons living with dementia.

Chapter 61:
Work within your loved one's reality

A delusion is a false belief that persists in spite of evidence to the contrary; an idea or object that is perceived incorrectly by the delusional person.

Dementia symptoms often include delusional thinking, meaning that the person with dementia may perceive things quite differently than they really are.

Within a world where what we see, touch, hear, smell, and believe can be validated by scientific observation, delusions are considered dangerous. Has anyone ever benefited from being delusional? Most of us would emphatically answer, "No!"

But the world we call "normal" can be quite different from the world of our loved ones living with dementia, and I am going to suggest that it is not always helpful for care partners to dismiss, deny, or denounce their delusional beliefs and behaviors.

People with dementia can totally lose recent memories, but may have strong and even accurate memories of an earlier time in their life; frequently during their early adulthood. While our reality remains grounded in the present, theirs becomes a facsimile of their past. As care partners, when we see evidence of this, we should not treat it as a dangerous or harmful delusion, but remind ourself that their reality is as real to them as ours is to us.

By trying to understand their reality and work within it, we can actually help our loved ones living with dementia. Rather than correct their misconceptions and argue about what is "real," try to enter their reality and encourage them to talk about it. This is what we call Validation Therapy. Don't argue; agree. Don't correct; validate!

I know of a woman in a memory care community who spent many hours each day talking to herself in a mirror. Rather than feel pity for this "delusional" behavior, the staff spoke with her and learned that she thought she was talking to her sister. They also noticed that she seemed most happy and calm during and after these conversations.

Her behavior was doing no harm, so they did not discourage it. In fact, when she seemed anxious or agitated, they took her to the mirror to talk to her beloved sister. By indulging her "delusion," they protected her dignity and elevated her quality of life.

A care partner's task is not easy. We must be grounded in our own reality to keep our loved ones safe and secure, but we must also understand and enter their reality to validate their beliefs and feelings.

As the health of our woman in the story declined, finally she could no longer walk and had to be placed in a wheel chair. When this happened, the understanding staff of her community lowered the mirror on the wall so she could continue to enjoy wonderful conversations with her sister!

This, my friends, is not delusional thinking. It is truly compassionate care. And care should be compassionate because we all deserve the best.

Chapter 62:
Handling hallucination

Hallucination can be one of the most difficult challenges a care partner for an individual living with dementia can face.

A hallucination is a sensory experience that appears real, but is fully created by the mind. It is not the same as a delusion, which is a misinterpretation of fact. For a hallucination, there is no factual basis. And it is not only visual; it can also be heard and smelled by the person experiencing the hallucination.

The occurrence of hallucinations can be a useful tool for properly identifying different forms of dementia. For example, hallucinations appear much more frequently in Lewy Body Dementia than in Alzheimer's, and some of the psychotropic meds prescribed for Alzheimer's disease can make Lewy Body hallucinations worse. So, the presence of hallucinations is a good indication that you should see a psychologist or neurologist who has experience in this field.

But diagnosis and medication aside, what do we do when hallucinations arise? These moments can be frightening for a care partner because they know they are dealing with a total fabrication of the mind.

There are two rules of care that apply. The first is the principle of Validation Therapy that teaches us that we should never deny, discount, or ridicule our loved one's reality. The second is to try to step fully into that reality and ask the kind of non-judgmental questions that let your loved one describe what they are experiencing. Remember that their reality is as valid to them as yours is to you!

None of this is easy, but let me share a true story told by a member of one of my care partner support groups.

One evening, she was sitting on the couch with her husband with dementia, eating apples and watching television. Out of the blue, her husband said, "I think there are Russians in the house!" She responded, "Are they wearing their uniforms?" Her husband leaned forward from the couch to get a better view, and said, "No, I don't think so. What do you think they want?" His wife responded, "Maybe they just want to eat some apples, then they will leave." Her husband said, "Oh, okay," and sat back to eat his apple and watch the television. Not another word was uttered about the Russians!

I thought this was absolutely brilliant. Notice that the care partner did not challenge the hallucination. She stepped fully into it and asked a factual question. This validated her husband's reality and began a conversation.

When he wondered why the Russians were there, his wife brought the discussion right back to their reality . . . Apples! This connected the Russians' intentions to something "normal" and totally non-threatening. End of discussion!

What do you think might have happened had she said in a scolding voice, "Oh, stop it, there are no Russians here!" The reaction likely would have been an angry and protracted battle of realities that could have ruined the evening.

Granted, this is not easy. One must have experience and be quick-witted, but when done skillfully, a validating response can lower the anxiety and fear of the person with dementia, and possibly even eliminate the concern in his mind that created the hallucination.

We are talking about "normalizing" a hallucination, and that in itself is challenging idea, but it can be done.

Chapter 63:
Don't dis your loved one's abilities

Dementia creates such shocking changes in the ones we love, it is not surprising that we become fixated on the skills and abilities they are losing.

Often, as our loved one declines in skill and cognition, they become annoying. They seem to be always under foot, messing up something you have just put in order, asking the same question over and over again. I encourage care partners to view these disruptive behaviors as their loved one's attempt to communicate.

People with dementia often lose language skills, and may not even know what they want, but they clearly sense that their world is going wrong. They are frightened, and perhaps they even understand that they are no longer holding up their side of the partnership. The last thing they need at these moments is to be reminded or criticized for what they CAN'T do.

Shifting our focus to their abilities – the things they still CAN do – requires compassion, patience, and even practice. But if we can do it, both of our lives will be better.

A woman in one of my support groups complained that her husband was driving her crazy; always under foot and interfering with her daily chores, which had become even more time-consuming, thanks to his disease.

I told her, "He may be telling you that he wants to help. On an emotional lever, he may sense that he is no longer working with you like he used to."

She responded, "But he can't do anything. He no longer knows the difference between a screw driver and a hammer!" Her husband had been an engineer and had always loved to fix things and keep their property in perfect order.

I said, "I bet he can fold towels. Wouldn't that be helpful?" She looked at me with astonishment. "He wouldn't do that; he has never done that!" I persuaded her that she could lose nothing by giving it a try.

The next time we spoke, she said, "You won't believe this. He spent hours folding towels. They were perfect. Every corner was square and they were stacked perfectly!"

I reminded her, "Your husband was an engineer. An engineer wants things to be uniform and consistent. This is ingrained into his values, and on an emotional level, he still has that need to do things right. Now you have found something he CAN still do, and he

has done it better than you ever would have."
She agreed that this was true.

Net result: The towels were perfectly folded
and she gained several hours of respite without
his being under foot and demanding her
attention. I believe that people with dementia
can sense on an emotional level that
something is wrong; that they are becoming
less useful. When we can give them a safe
and useful task – no matter how simple – they
feel needed and you gain more private or quiet
time.

Let's not focus on the "dis" in "disability," but
rather on what remains. It is a compassionate
technique of care that can improve the quality
of life for everyone involved. Focus on abilities
because we all deserve the best.

Chapter 64:
Beware the dangers of dehydration

As the hotter days of summer arrive, those of us caring for a loved one with dementia must become more wary of the dangers of dehydration.

First, we must be aware that an individual living with dementia may experience sensory changes that will leave them unable to recognize that they are not taking in enough fluids. They may not feel well, but be unable to connect this feeling with dehydration or describe how they feel. We may note that they seem more fatigued, confused, or irritable, yet not connect this with a lack of water.

The Mayo Clinic recommends 15 cups of water a day for men, and 11 for women. A senior may require less, but this should not be an excuse to neglect fluid intake. If your loved one's urine is clear to light yellow, they are getting enough water. Darker yellow urine is an indicator of dehydration.

As summer arrives, your loved one may want to walk more or sit in the sun. These changes in behavior are good since they will result in more exercise and greater intake of Vitamin D. Encourage this behavior, but be aware that it will create a greater need for water. We must become more proactive in encouraging them to drink liquids. Just as we do with their toileting, we may need to set a timed reminder on our smart phone or watch to tell us that it is time to encourage them to hydrate.

It is likely they cannot do this on their own, due to a range of sensory changes caused by dementia. They may be losing peripheral vision, depth perception, and color discrimination, which will make it more difficult for them to see or recognize a glass of water you have set out for them.

They will lose manual dexterity, making it more difficult to pick up a glass or bottle and maneuver it to their lips. As dementia progresses, we may have to help them drink.

Try using red coloring with the water, red healthy juices such as cranberry juice, or red containers. Studies have proven that red is not just easier to see, but it actually stimulates the appetite. It can be more appealing than a glass of clear water.

Good hydration is not just about drinking water. High water content foods are also effective, and, fortunately, many of these become popular or more available in the summer months. Examples are cucumbers, celery, zucchini, watermelon, strawberries, spinach, grapes, and cauliflower. Also, try Jell-o or that ever-popular treat, ice cream. Eggs have good water content, and also provide easy-to-consume protein.

Avoid high-sugar energy drinks. They are designed for high-activity, perspiring, younger people. For a senior, they can result a dangerous level of sugar retention.

We too often take hydration for granted. Please practice good hydration, both for yourself and your loved one with dementia, especially when hotter weather arrives.

Chapter 65:
Compassion Fatigue

Suddenly, my care partner support groups are devoting a lot of conversation to "compassion fatigue."

Compassion Fatigue is the care partner's Post Traumatic Stress Disorder; the response to overwhelming stress caused by the difficulty of a task, especially when we are cut off from resources and respite, as we have been during this time of COVID.

Compassion fatigue is characterized by physical and emotional exhaustion, feelings of inadequacy, self-contempt, weight loss or gain, headaches, a reduced ability to concentrate, and even the loss of empathy for the loved ones who require our care.

The phenomenon was first recognized among medical workers in Vietnam, and the term "compassion fatigue" was coined in 1992 by Carla Joinson who observed and wrote about compassion fatigue in nurses.

But unlike battle fatigue, compassion fatigue can bring a unique burden of guilt and self-loathing. "How can I become fed-up with caring for someone I love? There must be something wrong with me; something lacking in my basic moral character or sense of humanity!" Asking ourselves these questions, we plunge into a downward negative spiral taking us to a place where we are no use to ourselves or the loved ones we are caring for.

The first step in dealing with compassion fatigue is to understand it and recognize when and why it appears. No, you are not a bad person. You are experiencing a predictable, common, and well documented phenomenon. What you are feeling may be frightening and awful, but it is normal. Be kind to yourself.

Do not conclude, "I must not be caring enough. I'll just have to try harder and do more of what I'm doing." To the contrary, it is time for a break from what you've been doing. Again and again, your support group has talked about the things you need to do to take care of yourself. Now is the time to stop just talking about those things, and start doing them. Ask for some help.   This is necessary to your survival.

Find support that can help you get away from your task and your person for a while. You may need more than just an hour here and there, but some days away from being a care partner.

Write a journal about yourself and your feelings. Writing your thoughts and feelings can improve your perspective, help you realize how hard you've worked, and justify what you are feeling. Exercise. Adopt a healthier diet. Document your self-care behaviors in your journal. Get a lot of rest. Do not self-medicate.

There is a lot of information about compassion fatigue on the internet. Let me suggest https://www.aafp.org/fpm/2000/0400/p39.html.

You are not alone. I doubt that I know many care partners who are NOT experiencing compassion fatigue to some extent during this difficult time in our lives. The important thing is to prevent progress into a danger zone!

And remember my favorite slogan: We all deserve the best!

Chapter 66:
Communicating with
a person with dementia

Successful communication is a special challenge when we are caring for a loved one with dementia.

The best foundation for communication with a person with dementia is compassion. We must understand that they are coping with cognitive and sensory deficits, but we must also understand that they are still functional on an emotional level. Their "feelings" are very much intact, and how they respond to what we say depends to a great extent on how we make them feel.

Here are a few tips for effective communication:

Try to use statements rather than questions. People with dementia first lose their short-term memory, and even the simplest question that puts their memory to the test can seem confrontational. Instead of "What did you have for breakfast?" try saying "I bet you had a nice breakfast." They may just agree, or if they remember, they may tell you all about it.

Questions should be brief, without choices. If you must ask questions, try to avoid too many options. Don't say, "Would you like steak or chicken tonight?" This requires a choice, which suggests they can make a wrong choice. On an emotional level, they understand this and do not want to make mistakes. Try saying, "I'm having chicken. I bet you would like that too." And nod your head to encourage agreement. If they don't agree, they are likely to just tell you so, and then you can propose another option.

Do not repeat. If a statement or comment seems to confuse them, repeating it is likely to just make things worse. Slow down and try to make your point in a different way.

Keep it simple. Your person's auditory intake may be impaired. They may hear constant white noise and find it difficult to determine the direction from which a sound came. Also, their cognitive ability to process what they hear may be impaired. For example, a person with dementia may miss one out of every four words, so make your statements as brief and simple as possible.

Speak slowly. A person with dementia cannot process incoming information as quickly as you can. Speak slowly, and maintain eye contact to see if you are getting through.

Never contradict or argue. Your person is living in a different reality, but it is the only reality they have. When they say things that don't fit your interpretation of the world, just go with it. Validate their thoughts and feelings. You will gain nothing by trying to make them see things your way.

Don't talk "down" or use baby talk. You are communicating with an adult. Do not patronize, use baby talk, or otherwise treat them like they are a less whole human being than you. Their emotional structure remains intact, and they can sense this kind of treatment. It is demeaning and an affront to their dignity as an adult.

Communication is an art; not a science! Keep reminding yourself that dementia care is an art, not a science. Because our loved ones with dementia keep changing with the progression of the disease, our challenges as care partners keep changing as well. What worked yesterday may not work today. But this does not mean you failed or made a mistake.

Just keep following the principles of patience and compassion, and look for ways to connect with your loved one; not on a rational level, but on an emotional level. Keep trying, and keep reminding yourself that we all deserve the best.

Chapter 67:
Managing expectations

As we hope for the decline of COVID, all of us are looking for opportunities to return to "normal," which often includes travel. It is no different for care partners and their loved ones living with dementia, except for them traveling can present greater challenges.

Recently, I got a call from a member of one of my support groups who had just traveled to a northern state. She told me she thought everything was going well, until the day after her arrival when she experienced a complete emotional melt-down. She said she didn't see it coming, and was confused that it had happened.

I asked about details of the trip and learned that they had departed Florida late in the day, which created a problem finding a room, where they discovered they had left behind medications and dog food. Turns out, they were traveling not with a mature dog, but with a puppy! Their trip covered 1,200 miles over a four-day period, which included stopping to attend a funeral. In addition, our friend who solely managed this journey, including caring for her husband with dementia, is 80 years old!

Wow! This would have been a daunting and trouble-fraught task for a person half her age, and I was quite puzzled that she was puzzled that she had paid an emotional price.

I think the lesson here is that some of us may make assumptions that the "new normal" will be just a continuation of life as we knew it before COVID. Believing this, we think we can jump back into life as we knew it, and as we previously managed it.

I don't think we can. First, as care partners we have all aged during a time of our lives when aging can bring on significant changes, including decline in our physical abilities. Second, our loved one with dementia has likely declined more than they would have over the same period without COVID. We have seen clear and frequent evidence of this!

I believe it is healthy and important for us to get back into the world, but I wonder if we should greatly moderate our expectations. We can do this by planning to take on less than we think we can handle. We can always ramp up our plans and responsibilities, but not fulfilling them can lead to the kind of emotional toll my friend experienced.

Find ways to ease back into a semblance of your previous life. Don't make assumptions that you have your pre-COVID strengths and abilities. Pace yourself and watch closely for signs that you may be taking on too much.

As for travel, it has always been a serious challenge for families living with dementia. It is never easy. But there is plenty of good guidance out there. For example, check out the suggestions on Teepa Snow's web site at https://teepasnow.com/?s=travel+planning.

And continue the support group connections you have made during COVID. Even when you travel, arrange your schedule to check in with the others who care about you. None of us should try to manage dementia alone. And all of us deserve the best!

Chapter 68:
Should we care
about stages of dementia?

Many people think their understanding of dementia depends on knowing what "stage" their loved one is in. On average, dementia lasts eight to 12 years between diagnosis and death. It is progressive, irreversible, and fatal since no cure has yet been developed. But the symptoms and progress of dementia can be unique to the individual, often defying any tidy organization into "stages."

First, there is no single system to identify stages of dementia. Some dementia practitioners say there are three stages, some say four, and some say there are five. Perhaps the most widely recognized scale among neurologists is the Global Deterioration Scale developed by Dr. Barry Reisberg in 1983, which identifies seven stages. But then there is FAST -- the Functional Assessment Staging Test – that subdivides these seven stages into 16! Confused yet?

I can understand how these analytical approaches to categorizing the progress of mental and physical deterioration caused by dementia can be helpful for scientific research into therapies that can improve quality of life, but how can identifying and talking about the "stages" possibly help our care partners who struggle daily with real-world dementia? Your assigning your loved one a "stage" does not make him or her feel any better; nor does it make your task any easier.

I believe that focusing on the so-called "stages" of dementia is at best irrelevant to good care, and at worst detrimental to a care partner's emotional health and wellbeing. Not only can it paralyze the care partner with fear when they must look down that long road of future "stages," but it also can cause them to focus on the medical aspects of the disease – which they can't do anything about -- rather than the immediate quality of life of the person they are caring for.

In short, talking or worrying about "stages" gets in the way of our living in the moment and focusing on the quality of life of our loved one in the here-and-now, rather than what they are going to be like at a later "stage" of the process.

I am all for care partners knowing as much as they can about the medical aspects of Alzheimer's disease and other forms of dementia, but not if it distracts them from seeing their loved one as a human being who is experiencing real suffering that cannot be relieved one bit by wrapping it in a label that defines and numbers it as a "stage."

We know there are going to be changes as the disease progresses, but fixating on when they will come and what they will look like takes us out of the moment and distracts us from helping our loved ones through the process with compassion, empathy, and understanding.

And if thinking about stages seems important to us, let's remember that whatever stage we are in, we all deserve the best!

Chapter 69
Alzheimer's and Violence;
A common misconception

Often, when I am counseling a family that has just received an Alzheimer's diagnosis, someone will ask, "When will they become violent?"

This question reveals one of the most common and tragic misconceptions about the disease; that Alzheimer's leads to violent behavior; that their person will become unpredictable and dangerous.

It is true that one of the results of Alzheimer's – and many other forms of dementia – is personality change. But this change is not consistently toward violent behavior. If your person has a cooperative personality, this is likely to continue. If they have been difficult and combative, dementia is not likely to cause them to improve! But Alzheimer's does not invariably change a person toward unpleasant, confrontational, or violent behavior.

The misconception that Alzheimer's leads to violent behavior is too often caused by *US*, the care partners. It is the result of literally centuries of incompetent, unskilled, and misunderstood care. It is the result of how *WE* treat individuals living with dementia!

Everyone knows Alzheimer's causes memory loss. But what many don't know – including many care professionals – is that it also causes degradation of all of our cognitive and physical functions, including all five of our senses. I place great emphasis on this fact in my workshops because we cannot become effective care partners unless we learn to see, feel, and hear the world as they do.

What Alzheimer's does not attack equally is our emotional structure; our "feelings," our ability to experience joy, fear, pleasure, and pain. In fact, I believe that as the person's functional abilities change, their emotions become even more important. It is how they experience their world, and their fright-flight-fight response remains intact when they feel threatened or unsafe.

Too many people believe that a person with Alzheimer's eventually declines into a kind of vegetative state where they don't know what is going on. This is not the case. They still feel fear, confusion, and loss.

Care partners who do not understand their loved one's emotional capabilities too often treat them like a task; not like a fellow human being. We speak and move too quickly. We touch them without warning. We raise our voice in frustration because they do not respond as quickly as we think they should.

This approach leads to reactions we consider combative, but sadly, we are actually the ones provoking this unpleasant but predictable behavior. We victimize our loved ones without even realizing it. We blame them for both their behavior and our unskilled actions that caused it. This leads to a relationship of fear and distrust, which makes our care tasks even more difficult.

So, what can we do differently? Learn about the disease from a practitioner who believes in person-centered, compassionate care. Slow down. Speak slowly and lovingly. Make no physical contact without first making eye contact, and make eye contact with a smile. Verbalize love, praise, and validation. Never argue, correct them, or challenge their perceptions of reality.

Learn the skills and philosophy of hand-under-hand® management. Practice empathy and patience. And analyze your every move. If it gets a bad response, focus on yourself as the possible cause of that response rather than immediately blame your person.

People with Alzheimer's are not inherently violent. Let's not make them so. And like us, they also deserve the best.

Chapter 70:
Hogeweyk:
A model for compassionate care

November is National Alzheimer's Month. This will be used by many organizations to supercharge their efforts to solicit donations for a cure. Well and good, but I would like to see an equal level of enthusiasm directed toward funding to support family care partners and organizations that promote person-centered compassionate care. For those already in the journey, a cure cannot come soon enough.

I have just returned from the Netherlands where I spent two priceless days of learning at Hogeweyk, otherwise known worldwide as the Dementia Village. It is, in my opinion, a world-class model of best practices in person-centered care. Since its founding some 20 years ago, this organization has continued to seek, find, and implement better practices of compassionate dementia care.

The goal of Hogeweyk is to provide a "normal" environment. Seniors classified with severe to end-of-life dementia live in "villages/homes," not in little rooms in big buildings that look like hospitals, factories, or hotels. Hogeweyk simulates four different Dutch lifestyles, and residents are evaluated to live in the village that best duplicate the lifestyles in which they were raised and lived prior to dementia.

Because daily shopping for groceries is still a society-wide practice in the Netherlands, Hogeweyk has its own market where residents go each day to shop. There is a restaurant, but most residents eat in their own apartments which are carefully outfitted with the furniture, tableware, and decorations consistent with their "lifestyle."

It is a gated community, but not locked down. Residents are free to go where they choose, but wandering outside rarely happens because they are comfortable and have what they need in the environment that has been created for them. Hogeweyk is studiously maintained to NOT look anything like a hospital or health facility. Care staff do not wear scrubs; rather they wear normal street clothes with no name tags.

"Normalcy" is so well maintained that people come in from the town to enjoy Hogeweyk's restaurant, which helps supplement the community's income. Sometimes, it is a bit difficult to tell residents from the visitors. And among the residents, I saw very few using wheelchairs. Most residents are mobile, spending their time outside, in social activities, or interacting with the people of the community.

My mind is still spinning from this experience, trying to process the things I saw that were so different from the kind of senior care we are used to. I expect I will be sharing more of my thoughts about Hogeweyk in future columns.

Could these techniques of person-centered compassionate care be implemented on a national scale through our system of institutional care? I don't know, but I think we should be doing everything we can to find out. This is why we recently created in Citrus County a nonprofit organization with the stated vision to create an institute for researching, teaching, and promoting techniques of compassionate care, including nonpharmacological therapies.

It does work; I've seen it work. And I believe pursuit of the methods I've seen at Hogeweyk is the best way we can use the resources we have until someone comes up with that illusive cure.

For me, Hogeweyk seems to embody my belief that we all deserve the best.

Chapter 71:
How Hogeweyk
"normalizes" dementia

Last month, my column was about my recent visit to the Netherlands for a tour and workshop at Hogeweyk, famously known worldwide as the "Dementia Village."

The first thing I learned was that no one ever refers to Hogeweyk as a "dementia village." This is the term Sanjay Gupta coined some five years ago in his visit and story for CNN. Gupta used that term so his American audience would quickly grasp what he was talking about. But not only do the managers not use the term; they really don't like it!

Their choice to avoid the term "dementia village" reflects their essential commitment to an atmosphere and practice of "normalcy" in their environment and techniques of dementia care. They are not hiding what they do. They are not ashamed of it. They simply believe that NOT separating people living with dementia from the world in which they grew up is the key to better care and quality of life, and this belief permeates how they think and everything they do.

For example, the people at Hogeweyk actually laughed when one in our group used the term "pet therapy." We could tell from the blank stares among our delegation that something was going on that we did not understand.

Then they gently explained, "Do you use the term 'pet therapy' when little children respond well to animals? No, they simply love animals! It is a natural human response. There is no 'therapy' to it. It is the same with people with dementia. Our need to think of their natural love of animals as some kind of 'therapy' that we dementia practitioners recently discovered is an example of us setting them apart from the rest of the world, whether we realize it or not."

This is why, as I mentioned in my column last month, their care staff do not wear scrubs, uniforms, or even name tags. They are just people living in the village with their friends with dementia. As I began to gasp this concept, I began to notice how hard they try at Hogeweyk to pursue normalcy in every little detail.

I also mentioned last month that Hogeweyk has an open gate, but very little trouble with wandering. This is because their residents are comfortable where they are. There is nothing unfamiliar to alienate or frighten them, so they feel little reason to "escape." Hogeweyk actually encourages mobility, which is not the case in too many of the dementia care facilities in our own country.

Here in America, we certainly grasp this concept of "normalcy," but we have not yet even begun to dip our toe into the water. For example, we place familiar objects in the rooms of our residents living with dementia, but the moment they leave their room they step into the hallways of a medical factory.

Yes, I use the term "factory!" Our medical care has evolved from the concepts of efficiency and replication spawned by the industrial revolution. This may work well for many kinds of physical illness, but it does not work well for diseases of the mind when change and unfamiliarity can be confusing and frightening.

I wonder if we harm our loved ones with dementia even more by toying with little tokens of nostalgia and familiarity in parts of their environment, then thrusting them into common areas that are similar to the emergency rooms of hospitals or the lobbies of hotels. Surely this must be confusing and jarring to minds that are already struggling to understand why, who, and where they are.

Chapter 72:
Television; Friend or foe
of dementia care?

In today's world, the talking screen had become ubiquitous. It talks to us in our doctors' offices, it entertains us with sports at bars and restaurants, and it comes on to sell us something even when we pull the handle on the gas pump! It is a fact of life that we seem unable to avoid.

I have noticed also in both professional memory care facilities and in care partners' homes, the talking screen is ever-present. Is this good? Does it aid or detract from good dementia care?

I look at television as a tool, and like any tool it can be very helpful or extremely damaging, depending on whether we use it skillfully or haphazardly.

In determining how we use television, we must pay attention to the facts that 1) our loved ones with dementia process incoming information more slowly, if at all; and 2) they can have adverse reactions to too much visual and audio stimulation.

Too often, I visit homes or care facilities where people with dementia are sitting in a recliner, facing a big screen broadcasting 24-hour news.

This, in my opinion, is the absolute worst use of television. Cable news has an excited fast-talking head that suddenly switches to a different talking head. A moving image is dancing in the background, boxes with additional images are popping in and out of the corners of the screen, and across the bottom are scrolling banners that contain information that even the quickest-witted person cannot keep up with.

It is overstimulation on steroids, and in no way is it appropriate for a person with dementia. Not only does it over-stimulate, but our person with dementia cannot tell whether the latest bombing or shooting that the talking head is breathlessly describing is taking place in another city or right outside, on their own street.

My unequivocal advice is: Don't use cable news to baby sit your loved one with dementia. It is the equivalent of cruel and unusual punishment!

But this doesn't mean all television is bad. There are shows that can create a calming effect, which can be both appropriate and helpful. Certain forms of sports, such as tennis, baseball, or golf seem to sooth a person with dementia. They may have no idea who is playing, winning, or losing, but the repetitive motion of the game seems to have a calming effect. But avoid the kind of sport shows that focus on over-excited, loud, shouting announcers. Again, avoid the talking heads.

Movies can be beneficial. Movies that are nostalgic for your person, or that contain beautiful landscapes, quiet dialogue, or soothing music can work well. My husband dearly loved musicals. I wasn't too excited about watching "The Sound of Music" for the hundredth time, but it always calmed him, resulting in a smooth and peaceful transition to bed each evening.

There are now special television services designed specifically for seniors or families living with dementia. Uniper TV offers free interactive programming aimed at the interests of senior viewers. To learn more, go to https://www.unipercare.com. And Zinnia offers a subscription service intended specifically for individuals living with dementia. Check it out at https://www.zinniatv.com.

As dementia practitioners, we often advise care partners to avoid the overstimulation of television, but this does not mean it is inherently bad. Television is simply a tool that you can use for good or ill. Used wisely, it can give a care partner many hours of respite, and his or her loved one hours of tranquility. Like

other aspects of dementia care, with the use of
television we all deserve the best!

Appendix A
What is a Care Partner?

When the series of essays published here began in 2016, the term "care partner" was not in common use within the senior care industry. Rather, the common term for individuals providing care was "caregiver;" the one who gives care! It just makes sense, right? So why did we think the change to "care partner" important enough to become one of the few edits we have made throughout this book.

The term reflects not just the emergence of an important methodology of care, but also a core philosophy reflecting the relationship between a person living with dementia and the individual providing their care.

As a "caregiver," we think of ourselves as the person on whose shoulders the full burden of care falls. We think it our endless task to do things *for* or do things *to* the individual with dementia. It is a lonely and difficult task that is both demoralizing and exhausting. This attitude toward the care partner's role derives from the belief that individuals living with dementia can't do much of anything on their own, so what choice do we have but to do everything for them?

The term "care partner" challenges this view by encouraging those in the role of providing care to use a methodology and philosophy that seeks to recruit their person with dementia to become a participant and helper in most or all of their activities of daily living. One does not just care for the other. They look for ways to do it together.

Essential to the success of the care partner is a methodology of voice, approach, and touch that invites the person with dementia to respond and participate. This methodology is foundational in the teachings of Teepa Snow's Positive Approach to Care®. How we speak to, approach, and touch our individual living with dementia is critical to avoiding conflict, triggering so-called "behaviors," and achieving beneficial results that will not just get the task done, but protect the dementia person's dignity and self-esteem.

The role of care partner relies heavily on a technique of contact and physical support that we call Hand-under-hand®. The success of the Hand-under-hand technique comes from a lifetime of "muscle memory" developed by both parties, plus a powerful neurological connection between the heel of the thumb and one's brain that results in feelings of trust, comfort, pleasure, joy, and love. The method of contact helps the person with dementia feel that they have succeeded in a given task, which results in their feeling good about themselves and their relationship with their care partner.

Instructional videos for Hand-under-hand can be found on Teepa Snow's website and elsewhere on the internet. It is taught through instruction and role-play in all of Coping with Dementia's ABC of Dementia workshops.

Adjusting our methodologies of care in ways that recruit our loved ones to actively participate in all or most of their activities of daily living enables us – the care partners – to alter our attitude in positive ways that change the concept of our loved one from a burden of care to a partner in care. Emotionally, the method and the philosophy are beneficial for both parties.

Adoption of the term "care partner" is not just a semantic change. It reflects a philosophy of care that is more fulfilling and less burdensome for both parties, contributing to a better quality of life for each.

Appendix B:
Coping with Dementia LLC;
A Brief History

Debbie Selsavage was introduced to dementia when her husband Albert was diagnosed with Alzheimer's disease in 2005. When she asked the diagnosing physician what lay ahead, he simply stated, "Hang on for the Ride," and walked her to the door. Three years later, she was told that Albert had been incorrectly diagnosed, and that he had Parkinsonian dementia and possibly vascular dementia as well. This seemed par for the course: a disease that the medical community seemed to know little about, made worse by a lack of information, social services, and affordable care.

During their journey, Albert was twice Baker-acted*, hand-cuffed, placed in four-point restraints, physically beaten in a Baker Act facility, and kept for twelve weeks in a psychiatric ward . . . all because he had dementia. Fortunately, the journey ended better when Selsavage discovered a small, private memory care community that practiced what she would later learn to call "person-centered compassionate care."

Albert spent his final months in peace and serenity, now medication free and loved by people who used hugs rather than drugs. Selsavage wanted others to know there were correct and incorrect ways to care for loved ones with dementia, and after Albert's death in 2010, she entered the memory care field, vowing to practice the better way.

Moving into memory care

As a Florida-licensed assisted living administrator, she refined her understanding and skills in compassionate care and earned a Deficiency Free rating during her first year on the job. During this time, she met and formed a committed relationship with Ed Youngblood, a retiree from a 35-year career in nonprofit management and communications, whose mother died from Alzheimer's disease in 2008.

With a desire to reach beyond her 24-bed community with her message of person-centered compassionate care, Selsavage decided to organize a free conference for families living with dementia. Youngblood and Selsavage both had been dissatisfied with research-oriented conferences where experts lamented in their best medical jargon that they had not yet found a cure, but spoke little about care. They wanted something that spoke to average people, in plain language, and they named it the Coping with Dementia Family Caregiver Conference, scheduled for September, 2014.

Selsavage had no idea what to expect, and was astonished when 200 people arrived. She had chosen speakers to talk about caregiving – not research – and assembled a "resource room" with a dozen tables of private and county organizations that offered useful services and information.

The conference was a resounding success, and Youngblood said, "It is time for you to resign your job and create your own company. You cannot fulfill your vision running a 24-bed community." Selsavage resigned her administrator position that evening, and they set out to create Coping with Dementia LLC. Selsavage would become the face and voice of the company, and Youngblood would take on communications, curriculum development, and marketing strategy.

Creating the company

The venture was officially launched in April, 2015 with the ambitious but simply-stated mission to "Make life better for individuals living with dementia." The language "living with" was intended to apply both to individuals with dementia as well as their families and care partners.

During the winter months of 2014/15, the upstart business partners studied to become Certified Dementia Practitioners, and Selsavage further pursued certifications as a

Consultant and Independent Trainer in Teepa Snow's highly-respected Positive Approach to Care®.

The primary role of Coping with Dementia LLC is to educate. Selsavage wanted to promote an open and vigorous public conversation about dementia; to take the topic out of the shadows of shame, myth, fear, and misinformation. Specifically, she wanted to educate families and care partners in the practices, principles, and philosophy of person-centered compassionate care.

While her methods of care would be beneficial to anyone involved in dementia care, Selsavage decided to focus her attention on the family care partner community because she knew that 80 percent of Americans either cannot afford professional care, or prefer to keep their loved ones at home. This proved to be a correct business choice because few professional care communities have shown any interest in training their staff beyond minimum state standards, which are, in Florida, now almost 20 years old!

Coping with Dementia's mission to educate has emerged in three components: 1) Care partner education that has taken the form of the company's signature two-hour workshop entitled The ABC of Dementia, plus counseling and consultation; 2) Public education, that has resulted in a busy public speaking schedule and a traveling Alzheimer's and dementia awareness exhibit; and 3) Media, which includes print media, digital social media, and local television appearances.

The first ABC of Dementia workshop was conducted in July, 2015. Still popular today, its curriculum is based on the Positive Approach to Care®, including role play of the techniques of hand-under-hand® management; Naomi Feil's Validation Therapy, and practices of compassionate care that Selsavage developed while managing a memory care community. To date, more than 5,000 care partners in Florida's Nature Coast Region have attended the workshop.

As part of its public education initiative, in 2017 Coping with Dementia created an exhibit of 24 portraits of famous Americans who are living with or have succumbed from dementia. It includes well-known authors, artists, athletes, musicians, politicians, and entertainers, plus didactic panels containing facts about Alzheimer's disease and other forms of dementia. Its purpose is to convey factual information about the progressive and fatal nature of the disease, and to drive home the point that no one, regardless of race, gender, nationality, wealth, intelligence, or privilege is immune to dementia.

This exhibit has traveled to libraries in four west-central Florida counties, and during its life has grown from 24 to 54 portraits. To date, it has been viewed by an audience of more than a million people.

Also in 2017, the company added fund-raising to its mission, first on behalf of a regional organization that has now become defunct, then later to benefit Dementia Education Inc., which was formed in 2018 to focus on care partner needs in Citrus County.

Expanding from care to community service

While originally aimed at the needs of family care partner's, Coping with Dementia's ABC of Dementia curriculum can be modified to address enhanced customer and public service within the community at large. This application has launched a certification program whereby churches, businesses, gated communities, and government agencies can sponsor training to become Certified Dementia Friendly. A reasonable fee is charged for businesses and professional care organizations, but all of Coping with Dementia's training for nonprofit organizations is provided *pro bono*.

Citrus and surrounding counties have responded well to Coping with Dementia's program. During its first half-year of operation, the company made educational presentations to 19 organizations with a combined audience of 690 individuals. 167 family care partners were trained through eight ABC of Dementia workshops, and 16 organizations were certified Dementia Friendly.

Over the next three years, demand for Coping with Dementia's services grew exponentially both in Citrus and surrounding counties, especially in The Villages, which has become a vigorous secondary market. Educational speaking audiences grew to 1,309, 1,589, and 2,051 in 2016, 2017, and 2018 respectively, and family care partner trained grew to 703, 1,172, 1,318 over the same three-year period. During this period, 44 more organizations were certified Dementia Friendly.

Stepping back for COVID
The first quarter of 2019 promised continuing growth, then all activity came to a halt with the arrival of COVID. Workshops ceased in April 2019, and throughout all of 2020 only a single training event occurred! Slowly, activity has returned, and by the end of 2021 began to approach pre-COVID levels.

Over its seven-year history, Coping with Dementia has conducted 258 educational events to a total audience of 7,612 people; 155 ABC of Dementia training events have been conducted with 5,365 people trained; and 80 organizations have been certified Dementia

Friendly. On average, more than 1,000 per year have attended educational events, and more than 750 per year have received training in person-centered compassionate care. And prior to COVID, Selsavage facilitated two care partner support group meetings per month, serving an estimated 360 family care partners per year.

Finding new opportunities

COVID, it turned out, had a silver lining, opening up new areas of service. For example, with no ability to conduct in-person care partner support groups, the company began to host virtual support groups through Zoom. This enabled Selsavage to conduct three two-hour support groups per week rather than the previous two per month. Zoom also removed the geographical boundaries and brought in participants from as far away as California, Oregon, and Ontario, Canada. Support group attendance per meeting also more than doubled.

Similarly, the annual Coping with Dementia Family Care Partner Conference went virtual in 2021. Rather than an on-site, one-day event for 200 people, the Conference was expanded to four days with 16 speakers from all over the nation and Teepa Snow providing opening remarks. An on-line registration of 777 participants included viewers from as far away as Australia and the United Kingdom. To our knowledge, it was, by an order of magnitude, the largest conference about dementia ever conducted in the United States with as many as 400 participants signed in to some of the sessions!

Fortunate timing for a friendly community

One might see Coping with Dementia LLC as a company that has benefited from forming in the right place at the right time. More than a third of Citrus County citizens are over the age of 65, which is double the Florida 65-plus demographic. Nearby is The Villages where more than 50 percent of the population are seniors, making better dementia care a vital interest in west-central Florida.

Citrus County has responded to Coping with Dementia's vision and mission with gratitude. In 2017, Selsavage was named a Citrus County Health Care Hero, and in 2021 she was recognized with a Pillar of the Community Award and a Key Elder Care Citizen of the Year Award.

But perhaps one of the most fortunate events in Coping with Dementia's history came late in 2015 when Selsavage and Youngblood met with the Citrus County Chronicle to discuss the creation of an annual special tabloid section about Alzheimer's and dementia. Rejecting the tabloid section idea as too expensive, the editors rather invited Selsavage to write a monthly column for the Chronicle.

Over time, other publications in the region noticed and asked permission to republish the Coping with Dementia column, and today it is read in five monthly publications; four print and one digital.

After six years, 50,000 words, and more than 70 columns, it has been consolidated into the contents of this book. We hope it will enhance Coping with Dementia LLC's mission to serve and educate care partners and individuals living with dementia everywhere.

www.coping.today

*The Baker Act is a 50-year-old Florida law that empowers judges, law enforcement officers, doctors, and other authorities to involuntarily incarcerate within a mental health facility any individual deemed to be a danger to himself or others. The Baker Act was written primarily for drug addicts, psychotics, and other mentally ill and incorrigible individuals considered a danger to society, and was never contemplated to be frequently used as a tool to manage dementia. With the growth of dementia in our population, the Baker Act has been more frequently applied to *individuals with dementia, which often results in unnecessarily cruel, violent, and abusive confinement among a younger and sometimes dangerous population. Some memory care communities have been known to use the Baker Act as a tool of convenience to the extent that the term "dumping" has been coined within the senior care industry to characterize the casual incarceration of individuals with dementia who are considered too much a nuisance to deal with. Individuals with dementia who have a Baker Act on their record are less likely to be accepted for appropriate, conventional care. By being caught up in the Baker Act, they have essentially been stigmatized by unfortunate circumstances that were beyond their control, or behavior for which they are not responsible. And as a result, they are less likely to have access to adequate care.*

Appendix C:
Dementia Education Inc.

Dementia Education Inc. is a Florida nonprofit organization formed in July 2018. Its mission is to advance the education and understanding of memory diseases in a way that improves compassionate care for individuals living with dementia, and to support their care partners. It pursues this mission by funding programs and publications designed to advance person-centered compassionate care, specifically within Citrus County, Florida. While its Articles of Incorporation do not prohibit activity outside of Citrus, at the present time its board of directors has chosen to focus resources toward local needs.

To maintain a clear focus on its stated mission, Dementia Education Inc's nine-person board is composed entirely of individuals who have personally experienced care partnering with individuals living with dementia, either in their own families or as administrators or staff of professional care communities.

Dementia Education Inc. has published books entitled "A Handbook for Dementia Friendly Congregations" and "Dementia and Firearm Safety." The "Dementia Friendly Congregations" handbook has been distributed to every faith-based organization in Citrus

County, some 20 percent of which have hosted dementia care partner training provided on a pro *bono basis* by Coping with Dementia LLC. The "Firearm Safety" booklet has been distributed free of charge to hundreds of people through gun enthusiast channels. "Coping with Dementia" is Dementia Education's third book.

Dementia Education Inc, has also created a public information campaign called the Citrus County Scent Kit Coalition through which it promotes the distribution of human scent preservation kits used to rescue individuals – including those with dementia – who have wandered and become lost. Through the cooperation of several agencies, including the Citrus County Sheriff's Office, the Citrus County Libraries, Find-M Friends Inc., and Coping with Dementia LLC, more than 15,000 scent kits have been distributed free of charge throughout the county.

Dementia Education Inc. has helped fund conferences in Citrus County. These include the Summit to Protect and Serve our Seniors, hosted by the Citrus County Sheriff's Office, and the Coping with Dementia Family Care Partner Conference, which during 2021 was presented virtually to an international audience of nearly 800 registered participants.

Dementia Education Inc. pursues a long-term vision to create within the Florida Nature Coast Region an internationally recognized center for research and learning that will focus on the study and advancement of techniques of person-centered compassionate care, including non-pharmacological therapies.

The stated values of Dementia Education Inc. are:

Education: We believe in the importance of continuous improvement in the pursuit of quality memory care.

Partnership: We will work collaboratively with our community to inspire one another to succeed.

Dignity: We believe that compassion and respect are essential to quality care.

Diversity: As dementia has no boundaries, we will strive to serve people equally in regard to gender, race, nationality, color, or creed.

Integrity: We will work with purpose, honesty, and transparency to be accountable to our community.

Dementia Education Inc.
www.dementiaedu.org
dementiaed@aol.com